BASIC CHIP CARVING

with **Pam Gresham**

Schiffer Publishing Ltd

4880 Lower Valley Road Atglen, PA 19310

Dedication

This book is dedicated to my family. To my husband Peter for his unending caring and optimism. To my son Kyle for his youthful inspiration. To my parents, Coy and Nelma Mandrell for their help and encouragement.

Published by Schiffer Publishing, Ltd.
4880 Lower Valley Road
Atglen, PA 19310
Phone: (610) 593-1777 Fax: (610) 593-2002
E-mail: Schifferbk@aol.com
Please write for a free catalog.
This book may be purchased from the publisher.
Please include $3.95 postage.
Try your bookstore first.

We are interested in hearing from authors
with book ideas on related subjects.

Acknowledgments

I would like to give special thanks to my husband Peter who has given so much of his time and energy to me and my career. He stays focused and enthusiastic. He has more energy than ten people. He does my woodworking for me, while keeping up with his woodcarving career. Thank you for all your help through the years.

I want to thank my son Kyle for his understanding of the scope of this project. He was very patient and thoughtful throughout this process.

I must thank my brother-in-law, Richard Price, for his unique woodworking ability. His ideas are fresh and innovative. His energy is overwhelming. His help has been invaluable. I also extend my appreciation to his wife, Jill, for her understanding and input. You are both wonderful people. I also must thank Richard for the help with my computer. I could not have written this book without him.

I thank Bob Mishmash for his organizational skills, help and inspiration.

I must say thank you to David Draves. Thanks for your recommendation, encouragement, and help. He and Woodcrafters, now located in Parkersburg, West Virginia, have been instrumental in the development of this project.

I have to acknowledge the people at Silver Dollar City. I would like to say a big "thank you" to this wonderful group of people for their energy and desire to hold the best festival in the country. Thank you for making me a part of it.

I also must thank my parents, friends, and neighbors for everything they did for me during this project.

Finally, I extend my sincere appreciation to Douglas Congdon-Martin, Peter and Nancy Schiffer, and everyone at Schiffer Publishing. They have made this project, as difficult as it has been, one of the most enjoyable experiences of my life. Their patience, caring, and hospitality were wonderful. Thank you so very much.

Preface

I chose to write this book because I believe I have the capacity to help people understand and execute the art of chip carving. My goal is to explain the fundamentals of chip carving in an uncomplicated format. I hope to inform and inspire the reader enough to work through the difficulties, and eventually become a proficient chip carver.

Chip carving, when executed by an accomplished carver, looks easy. I find that many people get frustrated quickly because they cannot pick up the knife and the piece of wood and create a beautiful design. Chip carving can be compared with playing the piano. When one hears a trained pianist play a concert piece, it not only sounds beautiful, but looks easy. We all know that the pianist spent not only hours, but years practicing the fundamental techniques, then learning to apply those techniques to wonderful pieces of music.

Chip carving also has fundamental techniques that need to be learned, understood, and practiced. Only then can one create a beautiful carving. The wonderful aspect of chip carving is that often the simplest design creates the most beautiful piece. A chip carver can begin by carving a very simple design on a project, and finish with a great degree of fulfillment.

Contents

Introduction

This book studies in depth the fundamental techniques of chip carving. It progresses from the easiest to the hardest cuts. I have included designs for projects after each exercise, hoping this will help you stay enthusiastic throughout the learning process. I have not included many specific projects in this book. I feel there are numerous woodworking projects in books and magazines that lend themselves to chip carving.

I talk to people from all over the country who want to learn chip carving. I feel a need for a book that really gets down to the basics. These people want to know exactly how to execute each cut. They need a reference book to turn to when they are having difficulty with a certain type of cut. It is impossible for a novice to look at a geometric design on paper and know what to do with that design. I know, I've been there. I know there are good teachers out there, I took a weekend seminar myself with Wayne Barton and found it invaluable. That does not help a person who cannot get to these teachers. Neither does it help the person that is carving and has a question that needs an immediate answer from an experienced chip carver.

I worked hard for two years to learn chip carving. My husband laughs and tells people that I carved the best firewood ever burned. I literally threw everything away for the first two years. I really wanted to become a proficient chip carver. I can remember becoming so frustrated that I threw the knife and declared, "I quit—no more." I'm sure my family remembers it too. When I calmed down I would pick up the knife and keep trying. Finally one day it started happening for me. Designs came out the way I wanted.

I hope this book eliminates the guessing and frustration for you. In it I show you my techniques. Others probably do not execute each cut the same as I do. I can only say that I have been a professional chip carver for many years now. I carve over two thousand pieces a year. Some pieces are small, others are large. People seem to enjoy and appreciate my work. I won the National Woodcarvers Showcase, Professional Chip Carving category for the past three years. Two years winning the First, Second, and Third ribbons and one year winning the First and Third places. No one loves chip carving more than I do. I try to carve every day, usually all day. I put in longer hours than I did when I had a "regular" job. I have not tired of carving yet. I love creating pieces that I know will be appreciated for many generations.

I enjoy the history of chip carving. Many designs we see today originated with the European peasants. These designs are very aesthetically pleasing. The peasants carved mainly on utilitarian items. I believe the aesthetic designs and the utilitarian aspect are the reasons that chip carving is seeing such a resurgence in popularity.

My work is usually on usable household items. I am lucky because my husband and brother-in-law are wonderful woodworkers. Whatever I can dream up, they can make. Almost everyone knows someone with a wood shop who is willing to make a project for them to carve. If not, craft shops and woodworking catalogs now sell items such as basswood boxes, plates, and breadboards, etc..

Chip carving is not only relaxing, but it is also addicting. This is not just my opinion, but the opinion of others I talk to from across the country. It has a calming effect, which I think is true with any form of carving. Because one chip carves on the lap, and uses only two tools, there is a great amount of freedom in choosing a place to carve. One can carve while relaxing in the living room, at the park, or anywhere else they choose to be.

I hope you spend many wonderful hours chip carving. Good Luck!

Selecting and Preparing the Wood

The selection of the wood plays an important role in chip carving. The type and quality of a piece of wood can make a definite difference in the outcome of a carving. A spongy piece of wood will cause the carver frustration because it will fold and crumble under the knife. It also will cost the carver time. The carving from this wood will never have a truly clean, sharp finished appearance. A good crisp wood, on the other hand, will make carving the pleasure it should be, save time, and allow the carver to create a clean, sharp carving.

Basswood, also known as Lindenwood, is the wood of choice for chip carvers. Basswood is more suitable because the grain is straight and even. Basswood is in the hardwood family, but it is the softer of the hardwoods. It is a stable wood. It tends not to warp because of its consistent grain. In my experience, there is a difference in the basswood grown in different climates. Basswood grown in the northern part of the country is more suitable for carving. Northern basswood is compact and dense because it grows slowly in a colder climate. Southern basswood has an open grain because it grows quickly. It feels spongy and stringy when carved. Northern basswood will appear much whiter than southern basswood. A good rule of thumb when picking out basswood is the whiter and lighter the wood, the better for carving it will be.

Chip carving can be done in the other woods also. I realize that some woodworkers will wish to embellish their projects in other woods with chip carving. The different woods should be used only after the carver has attained a degree of skill and is comfortable with the fundamentals of chip carving.

As I see it, there are two drawbacks to carving in different woods. The first drawback is that the inconsistency in the grain makes control of the knife much more difficult. The dark streaks are hard and the light streaks are soft. The carver must use more grit to get through the darker, harder streaks. Then before the carver knows it, they are through the hard streak and into the lighter, softer streak. This is where the knife will slip. It is hard to control the knife when going in and out of the harder and softer streaks.

The second drawback is that the randomness of the grain creates a visual conflict with the symmetry of a chip carved design. A carving done in wood with a heavy grain may seem confused and busy. The grain fights the design. Sometimes the grain can compliment a free form (non-geometric) design. To visualize the finished piece at the initial lay out stage, the designer/carver needs to have achieved a level of proficiency in designing and carving. This ability only comes with practice.

The beginning chip carver should carve in basswood. This wood will allow one to learn the fundamentals with a minimum of frustration due to the wood. A carver will inevitably run into bad pieces of wood. Sometimes the wood will be extremely hard, or it will not cut clean. It will not matter how sharp the knife is, or how much skill the carver has attained. Most of the time the carver will find basswood, particularly northern basswood, an excellent carving wood.

One can usually find basswood at a specialty hardwood store. Be sure the wood has been kiln dried. Because this drying process has removed most of the moisture, the wood will not warp or split later. Air dried wood will warp easily and will harden as it ages. If one buys air dried wood and leaves it sit, it will harden. Kiln dried wood is always the best choice.

Preparing the Wood

The wood has to be finish sanded before the chip carving design can be drawn on the board. The completed carving cannot be sanded. In a geometrically drawn design, the lines of the design will be left after the carving has been completed. The spaces between the lines will be carved away. If you sand on a completed carving, the sharp edges of the design will be flattened. This will take the clean, sharp look from the carving. To remove any pencil and design markings left on the carving, gently erase only. Some gentle hand sanding can be done around the carving, but the main sanding should be done before putting the design on the board.

Always sand the wood in the direction of the grain. Never sand across the grain. This will leave scratch marks on the surface of the wood. Any sanding marks left at this point will be brought out when applying the finish. The finish will magnify, not hide any flaws left at this preliminary stage. Look at the sanded piece under a bright light or in the sunlight, and from different angles. This will help you to see any sanding marks that might still be on the wood. After completing the sanding, it will be time to draw the design on the wood.

Tools

Tools needed for chip carving include both tools for drawing and tools for cutting.

Drawing Tools:

I. Mechanical pencil with soft lead.

II. Erasers—two types

A. Clic eraser (replaceable pencil type). Great for erasing in small places, or where only a single line needs to be erased.

B. Large rectangular pink eraser. Used on completed carving. Takes markings off the outside edges of the carving (rosettes, straight lines, etc.) where carving is not delicate and pieces will not easily chip out.

III. Rulers—two types

A. A quality thick plastic ruler marked in both inches and metric units. It helps to have these in different lengths.

B. A flexible clear plastic ruler. This helps when drawing on both dished and rounded surfaces. Also the clearness helps when it is necessary to line up certain lines, and to keep the very short lines straight—i.e., ¼" or 4 to 5 cm. You will understand this clearly when you start measuring.

IV. Drafting Compass—Make sure the compass is the type with the screw in the center so that the compass cannot slip after you set the distance. I like to have at least two of these because I use them to divide distances, as well as to draw circles. Most office supply stores will carry this type of compass.

V. T Square and/or a speed square.—These are invaluable tools for laying out patterns. After making the placement marks, you will use these to draw the lines. I prefer the speed square. It seems easier to handle because it is a little shorter. The more you use this tool, the more you will come to depend on it.

VI. Parchment paper.—This is a clear paper used to transfer designs.

VII. Wax Free Transfer Paper.—This is used to transfer designs. It is easily erased, almost easier than a pencil. This can prove very useful for both the novice and the advanced designer/carver. I use the Saral brand.

Carving Tools

I. *Chip carving knife.* I prefer the Swiss knives because they have shorter blades than most other knives. This length allows the carver to place the inside joint of the thumb on the bottom of the handle, while keeping the tip of the thumb on the wood. The carver controls the depth of the cut this way. The carver develops a "feel" for the depth with practice. There are German knives also. Each brand of knife is a little different. Do not be afraid to try different tools until you find one that is suitable for you.

There are two brand names of knives I will recommend:

A. The Barton knife. This is my favorite. It is a small knife and very easy to use.

The Swiss carving knife.

B. The Pfeil knife. This knife has a slightly longer blade. It is also a good knife.

II. *The stab knife.* This knife will be used very little. It does no cutting. It forms a small V-shape when pushed straight down into the wood. It embellishes the design and adds a new dimension to the carving.

The stab knife

Parts of a Knife

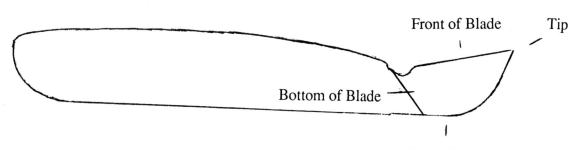

Front of Blade

Tip

Bottom of Blade

Back of Blade

III. *Tools for sharpening the knife.* There are several options. Many people already have a system they are happy with. If not, a discussion of some options, such as stones and wheels follow later in this chapter.

SHARPENING THE KNIFE

There are many methods for sharpening a knife. As I stated before, I meet people from all over the country when I am at the National Craft Festival at Silver Dollar City, Branson, Missouri. It seems many people have a particular method of sharpening they like to use. For those people, keep doing what you're doing. For the others who are having trouble, I will answer a few important questions.

When I began to chip carve, and continued to carve only as a hobby, I used ceramic stones to sharpen my knives. These stones can be found in stores and catalogs. There are two stones, the medium and the ultra fine. They are great for sharpening chip carving knives because they are dry stones that do not require water or oil. This eliminates any chance of getting water or oil on the wood after sharpening.

I do not use stones anymore for one reason: I find that sharpening with stones requires too much time. My husband is also a professional woodcarver. He carves in the round and relief carvings. He uses chisels, gouges, V-tools, and knives. We already had

the grinders to sharpen his tools. I began to use his grinders, and with him developed a method of sharpening my chip carving knife using an electric grinder.

Since the stones and the grinder are the two methods I am familiar with, these are the two I discuss. There are other ways, but I cannot discuss them since I have no frame of reference for them.

Sharpening with Ceramic Stones

There are two ceramic stones. The dark one is the medium grit stone, used to thin and shape. The white one is the ultra fine stone used to buff and polish.

A new knife needs to be thinned before it can glide through the wood easily. Use the medium (dark) stone. Look at the thickness of the knife. Note the taper from the front of the blade to the back of the blade. Think of the entire metal piece (from front to back) as "the blade." A chip carving knife does not have an "edge" like on a pair of scissors, a chisel, or a regular kitchen knife. The chip carving knife needs to glide through the wood easily. If there is an "edge," then there is a build up or thicker part behind the "edge." You do not want a build up behind the front of the blade. You want a straight, even taper from the front of the blade to the back of the blade. (Refer again to the drawing.) A build up makes moving through the wood much harder.

7

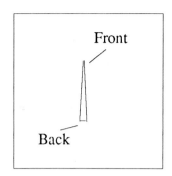

The cross-section of the blade.

When you look at the edge of the knife from the side in the light and move it around, you do not want to see any angles.

Therefore, lay the blade flat on the stone, tip toward the center of the stone and handle almost butted up to stone. Raise the back of the blade just a little, to a 10 degree angle. This is not much. If you raise too much you create the "edge" you do not want. Move the knife back and forth evenly across the stone. Put more pressure on the bottom of the blade (next to the handle) than at the tip. If you don't do this, you tend to take too much off the tip, thus rounding it. Flip the knife over and do the same. If you feel a burr, keep sharpening on one side, then the other (without much pressure) until the burr disappears.

When you think you have the blade thinned, and you can see no angles reflected in the light, it is time to polish the blade. Do this using the white ultra fine stone and in the same manner as already explained.

Lay the blade flat on the stone with the tip toward the center and the handle almost butted to the stone. Lift the back of the blade about ten degrees.

Use the ultrafine stone to polish the blade.

After polishing, check the knife by cutting with it. If it tears the wood, or just feels thick, keep sharpening. I find that after I sharpen a new knife and use it for a few cuts, it burrs. I expect this. I sharpen it again, and it is good for a long time. After the initial sharpening and polishing, you should use the medium stone only occasionally. Most of the time the knife only needs to be buffed.

Sharpening with an Electric Grinder

If you are a relief or an in-the-round carver, you probably use a grinder to sharpen your tools. You can use this method to sharpen the cutting knife. If you are not familiar with an electric grinder, be extremely careful. There are two major drawbacks to this method. The first drawback is safety. The grinder can flip the knife right out of your hands, and right back at you. I urge you to **use extreme caution** when using a grinder. Please wear safety goggles. The second drawback is the grinder removes the metal so fast that it is easy to ruin a knife.

The ideas pertaining to the sharpening of the blade remain the same. There are only certain rules for grinding to discuss at this point.

Use a 60 to 80 grit stone wheel. This grit removes the metal quickly, without letting the blade get too hot. The use of a finer grit removes the metal too slowly, thus allowing the blade to heat up. If a blade heats enough to turn blue, it probably will be ruined. This removes the temper from the metal. Never make two passes in quick succession. The blade needs to cool between passes.

To thin the knife, sharpen on either side (but only one side) until the knife burrs on the other side. Then buff on the same side you ground on until the burr falls off. Do not grind or buff from side to side because it breaks the burr off and leaves a flat edge on the knife.

When sharpening on an electric grinder, always start at the tip and grind toward the handle. Never pull from the handle to the tip. If you do, you push the heat to the tip, the thinnest part of the knife, and run the hazard of overheating the blade.

To buff or polish the blade after thinning or reshaping a used knife, use either a leather or hard felt wheel. The leather wheel is the best, but it is expensive and hard to find. The felt wheel works fine also, but do not use too much pressure. Do not allow the wheel to wrap around the blade. This rounds the blade and you do not want that. We use a buffing compound called "Zam." This puts a wonderful polish on the knife.

Sharpening the Stab Knife

I use the ceramic stones to sharpen the stab knife. It has an edge that is clearly visible. Put the stab knife on the stone at more of an angle than used for the cutting knife. It requires about a 30 degree angle. Rub the knife back and forth just as with the cutting knife. Polish the stab knife after you finish sharpening.

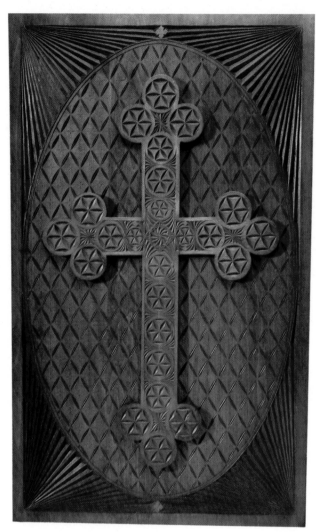

Excercise One
Carving a Single Triangle

Before we begin the following exercises I would like to explain how I intend to proceed. In the next part of the book I have tried to be very basic. I have assumed that the reader is not familiar with the execution of chip carving. The explanations seem long; they really are not. The exercises become very simple once you have read, tried, and practiced each. I have stated some information in more than one way so that it may be understood by all. I also have repeated some important or hard to understand information more than once. Following each exercise, I have summarized the information in a form that you can say to yourself while learning to carve each exercise.

Please do not get frustrated here. Work through your problems. Learning to carve will come faster than you think it will at first. It will be very satisfying. Once you understand the basics enough to execute a few simple cuts, the rest will quickly follow.

This method of study will allow the beginner to learn the fundamentals of chip carving, and help the more advanced carver to hone their skills. The ordered exercises will build your skill and knowledge of chip carving. I have begun with the most basic cuts and followed through to the most difficult.

We are going to begin by working on a practice board. It should be no larger than 8 ½ by 9 inches. Since it is only a practice board, this is only an approximate size. Use whatever size is available. This is a comfortable size to work with. If the board is small, too much time will be spent drawing the lines for the designs and less time carving. The board should be rectangular shaped for the purposes of the first exercise. The grain should run parallel with the shorter sides of the board. (Photo 1)

Begin by drawing a border line ½ inch in from each side. At this point we are only going to work on simple triangles. They are the basis of almost every chip carved design. It is imperative to master these first.

While you have the board in front of you at this point, letter the edges of the board as shown. (Drawing 1) These letters are to aid you when learning to cut each exercise. Be sure to copy the letters exactly as written. The reason will soon become apparent.

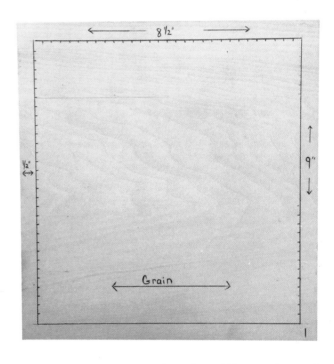

Photo 1: Note the grain direction, ½″ margin, and horizontal and vertical markings.

Drawing 1: The labeling of the sides of the board with letters. This will help you keep your place with the following directions. Sides A and B are opposite each other and go with the grain; sides C and D are opposite each other and are against the grain.

Photo 2: Mark ¼" measures.

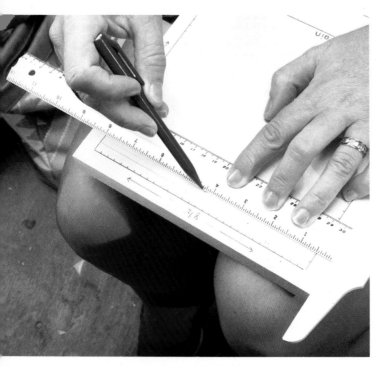

Photo 3: A T-square is used to draw lines.

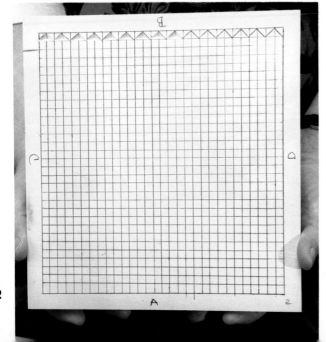

Photo 4: The ¼" grid.

To draw several triangles at once, the board needs to be laid out in a ¼ inch grid. (Photo 2) We will add the diagonal lines for the triangles after the grid is on the board. Lay your ruler on one horizontal border line and make a small mark at every ¼ inch line. Do the same with a vertical line.

Now use your T square, or speed square (whichever you prefer), to draw the longer lines across the board. (Photo 3) An easy way to do this is to put your pencil point on the ¼ inch mark and then slide the T square over until it hits the pencil. Draw the line. Go to the next ¼ inch mark using the same technique. Draw all the horizontal and vertical lines. This technique only works if the board is somewhat square with straight sides.

If it is not, you have to mark all four border lines in ¼ inch measurements. (Refer again to Photo 1) Then draw the long horizontal and vertical lines with a ruler. I know at this point that some readers have more experience than others. If you are a beginner, I would suggest that you go ahead and mark off the entire board. If you are at a higher level, you must decide for yourself how much of the board to mark off for this first exercise.

I must explain my method of measuring here. Chip carving, being a European craft, is usually in the metric system. I frequently use the metric system myself, but I have chosen to teach in the decimal system. I feel that most people learning from this book will be more familiar with the decimal system. It is confusing for people to try to learn the metric system, drawing, and technique all at once. I am concentrating on teaching the execution of the cuts for now. For the beginner, and people unfamiliar with the metric system, working in inches and divisions of inches is the quickest and easiest way to learn chip carving. I find that sometimes I want a certain look in a design, and can only get it using a metric measurement. For those who wish to use it, an explanation of drawing borders in the metric system follows later in this book.

You have your board marked off in a ¼ inch grid. (Photo 4) It is now time to mark the triangles. Only mark one row for now. It will be obvious how the rest of the rows should be spaced after you have carved a complete one. Then you can mark off several rows. Place the board with the grain running horizontally in front of you. (Photo 5) Mark off the top row of triangles. An easy way to do this is to mark all the diagonal lines in one direction first. (Drawing 2) Be sure to skip a square between each diagonal line. Next go back and draw the other side of each triangle. (Drawing 3)

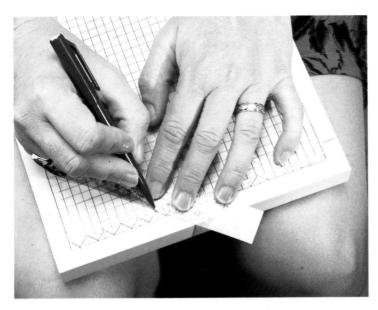

Photo 5: Draw diagonals on one line.

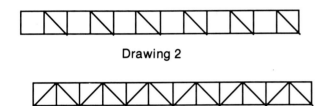

Drawing 2

Drawing 3

Before we cut, let's take a closer look at a single triangle and see what we are trying to do within that triangle. A drawn triangle looks flat. I want you to look at it from the standpoint of what your knife needs to do with this triangle. Here is an enlarged triangle with dotted lines marking the center bottom of a cut triangle. (See Drawing 4 on page 14)

Look at Photo 6 and Drawing 4 until you can see that the dotted lines would be at the bottom of the triangles. When cutting, the dotted lines would denote where the **point** of the knife needs to be inside the wood. This is the bottom, center of the cut. The tip of the knife will be here when cutting.

I have enlarged the triangle in Drawing 4 for study purposes. Think of this whole page as a single triangle on your practice board. I have plotted each cut on this diagram. It shows the start, direction, and end of each cut. It also shows the direction the board should face to execute each cut. It might be helpful to copy the entire illustration of the enlarged triangle at a copy machine. That way you can turn the paper while reading the text. The single sheet of paper would denote your practice board. I have lettered the edges the same as your practice board should be lettered. The large triangle should be facing the same way your smaller ones are on your practice board. Side A should be at the bottom closest to you and facing you. From now on I am only going to say that the letter should be facing you. Note that when Side A faces you, letter B is upside down. The same holds true for each opposing side.

Photo 6: A simple carved triangle.

Remember that the dotted line is the bottom center of the cut. It is where the point of the knife needs to be. When cutting try to concentrate on the point of the knife. You cannot see it, but imagine where it is in the wood. You do not want to cut too deep. Chip carving creates a contrast between light and dark. If your cuts are too deep, there will be only darkness in the cut, causing it to lose its effect. It will not have the angled sides leading the eye to the bottom of the cut, and then back out again.

Place the board on your lap. (Photo 7) To get the correct angle, chip carving should be done with the work on the lap. If your elbow is sticking out, push the board forward toward your knees. This automatically brings your elbow in toward your body. Position the board so it is comfortable.

Photo 7: The lap position for carving.

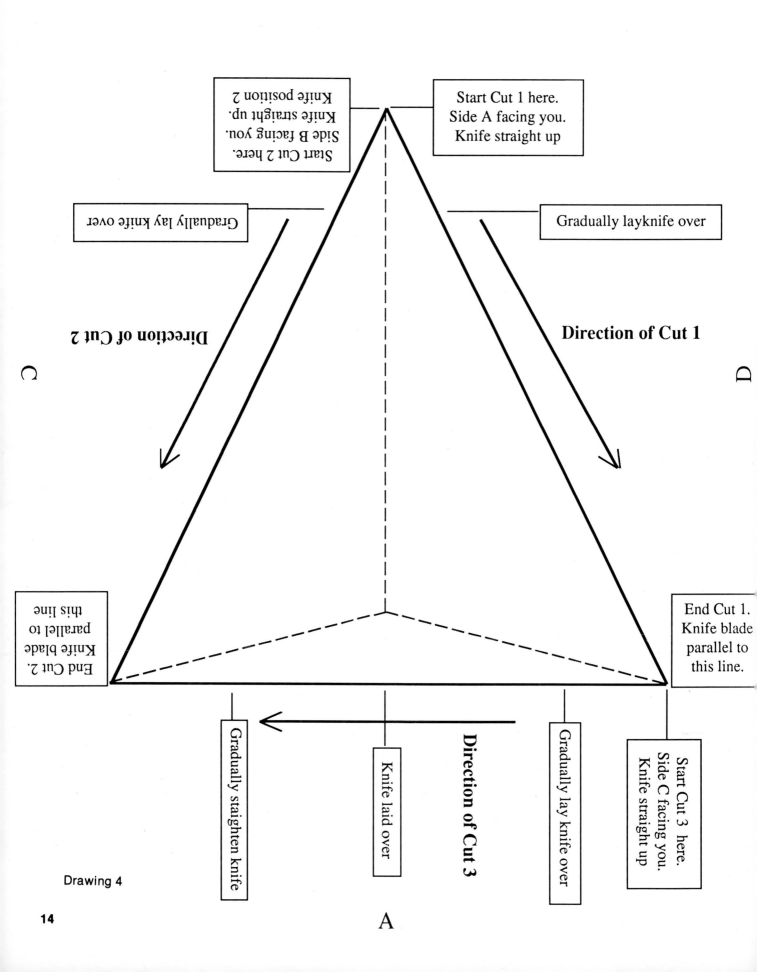

B

Start Cut 1 here.
Side A facing you.
Knife straight up

Start Cut 2 here.
Side B facing you.
Knife straight up.
Knife position 2

Gradually lay knife over

Gradually lay knife over

C

Direction of Cut 2

Direction of Cut 1

D

End Cut 2.
Knife blade
parallel to
this line

End Cut 1.
Knife blade
parallel to
this line.

Gradually staighten knife

Knife laid over

Direction of Cut 3

Gradually lay knife over

Start Cut 3 here.
Side C facing you.
Knife straight up

Drawing 4

14

A

When cutting a triangle there are two positions for holding the knife. These are the only two positions ever used in chip carving.

Position 1 (Photo 8): Used when drawing the knife toward you. Grasp the handle of the knife firmly with the blade facing you. The middle inside joint of your index finger should be where the back of the blade meets the handle. Keep the hand completely on the wood. The placement of the thumb is the tricky part, and the hardest to endure while learning. It is necessary to learn this correctly because it will keep you from slicing your thumb, and will eventually control the depth. The inside joint of your thumb should be placed at the very end of the wooden handle. (Photo 9)

The blade of the knife will be almost on your thumb. Now you have to bend your thumb slightly backward at the middle joint. Place the tip of your thumb on the board. Refer again to Photo 9. This will feel very uncomfortable and awkward at first. It will become

second nature with practice. It is necessary to learn this correctly. This is the position for 95% of chip carving. The relationship between the knife, thumb, and board is what will eventually give you the "feel" for the correct depth. The thumb and the knife will always stay together in this position.

Never pull the knife toward your thumb. You will positively slice your thumb if you do this. The knife and the inside joint of the thumb **always** stay together in Position 1. If the knife slips in the wood, the hand should go with it. A sore spot, and then a callus will appear on the thumb joint if you are holding the knife correctly.

Look at Drawing 4. Place your knife at the top point of the triangle. Notice where the dotted line is, at this point. It is close to the cutting line. You want your knife to be straight up and only slightly inserted into the wood. (Photos 10 and 11) If you angle the blade of your knife too far, or you insert it too deeply into the wood here, you will undercut the other side of the triangle.

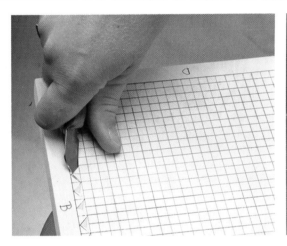

Photo 8: Knife or hand Position 1.

Photo 10: At the start of the triangle the blade is only slightly inserted into the wood.

Photo 9: The thumb position

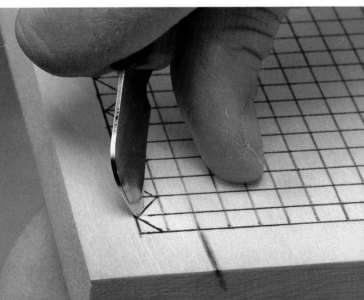

Photo 11: Keep the angle steep.

Start Cut 1. Remember to start with the knife straight up and shallow. Cut toward the direction of the arrow; toward your body. As you pull the knife toward you, gradually lay it over, and gently push it deeper into the wood as you go. (Photo 12)

Remember to think about the point of the knife. You want to cut into the middle of the triangle, or to the imaginary dotted line. Do not cut too deep or stay too shallow. The tendency here is to cut too deep. I find that I lay the knife over so that the knuckles of my index finger just barely touch the wood at the end of this cut. At the bottom of the triangle, as you finish the cut, your knife blade should look parallel with the line forming the bottom of the triangle.

The point of the knife will not reach the center of the triangle here at the widest part. (Photo 13) Remember you have to cut the bottom line yet. That is why in Drawing 4 the solid bottom line of the triangle, and the dotted bottom lines, form a small triangle. This denotes the cut across the bottom, which will be the last cut. You have completed cutting the first line of the triangle, Cut 1.

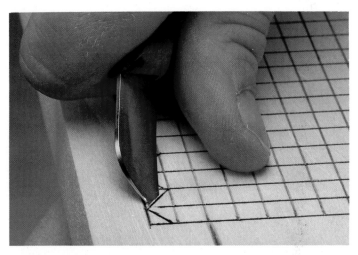

Photo 12: Lay the blade over as you progress down the cut.

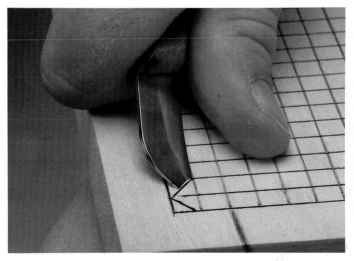

Photo 13: The end of Cut 1.

Refer again to Drawing 4. Cut 2 starts at the top of the triangle again, but with the board turned so the Side B is now facing you. You push the knife away from your body to make this cut. Therefore, the hand and the knife must be held in a different way. This is Position 2. (Photo 14)

To hold the knife in the Position 2, place the knife in your hand with the blade facing away from your body. Your thumb should be placed on the back of the knife with a little of the tip of the thumb (almost ½ inch) on the back part of the blade. Wrap the rest of your fingers firmly around the knife handle.

It is not physically possible to begin this cut with the knife straight up, but get it as up and down as possible. (Photo 15) Again, do not insert the blade too deeply into the wood. Remember, do not let your elbow stick out from your body. It will be the tendency here. Push the work further out toward the knees if needed to bring the elbow closer to your body. As you make the cut gradually lay the knife over and gently push deeper into the wood. (Photo 16) Remember do not cut too deeply. To end the cut, the knife should again be parallel with the line that forms the bottom of the triangle. (Photo 17) This completes Cut 2.

Now we are going to carve the last line of the triangle, Cut 3. Turn the board so Side C faces you. Return to knife Position 1. Execute this cut by pulling the knife toward you as in Cut 1. Note the dotted line in Drawing 4. The knife will be straight up and barely inserted into the wood at the beginning and end of this cut. (Photo 18) At the center it will be laid over and deeper. (Photo 19) Remember to think about where the point of the knife is in the wood. You need to look carefully at the diagram. Start the cut straight up and shallow. Gradually lay the knife over and deepen. Then after you have passed the center, gradually straighten the knife and take it out of the wood to end the cut. (Photo 20) This cut completes the triangle.

If the chip does not pop out immediately and cleanly, go over the three cuts again. The triangular chip should pop out this time. There may be some wood debris left in the bottom of the cut. Clean this out by following the original angles. To avoid having different angles in your triangle you must follow the original angles. (Photo 21)

Photo 14: Knife or Hand Position 2, used when pushing the knife away from body, Cut 2 only.

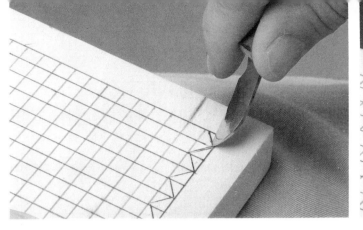

Photo 15: Beginning the second cut.

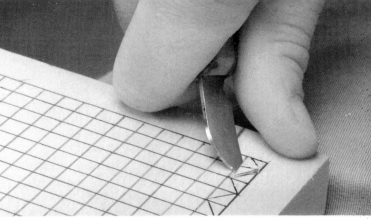

Photo 19: The middle of Cut 3.

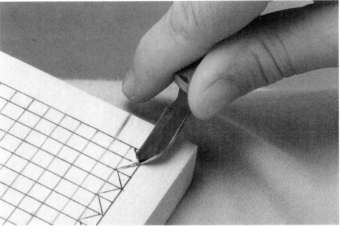

Photo 16: The middle of Cut 2.

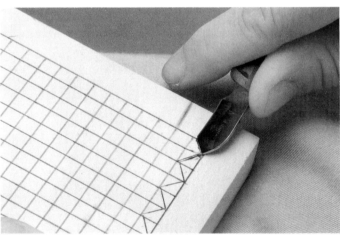

Photo 17: The end of Cut 2.

Photo 18: Begin Cut 3.

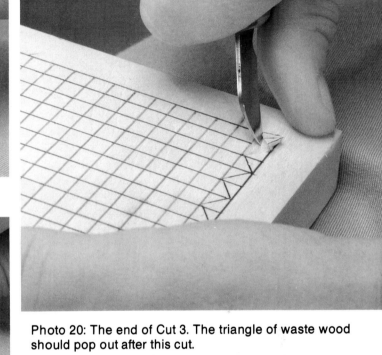

Photo 20: The end of Cut 3. The triangle of waste wood should pop out after this cut.

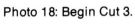

Photo 21: The finished triangle.

Summary of Exercise 1: Cutting a single triangle

I have written this summary so you can say it to yourself while executing the cuts. When I began to chip carve, I found knowing which way to turn the board, and the knife positions very confusing and frustrating. This summary is a simplification of the entire process. I have removed the confusion with the lettered practice board, the diagram of the enlarged triangle, and the following summary to read as you execute cutting the triangle. You should quickly master this exercise.

Cut 1: Side A facing me. Knife Position 1 (pulling toward body). Start cut at top with knife blade straight up, barely inserted into wood. Pull knife toward me while gently pushing knife deeper. Gradually lay the knife over until blade is parallel with bottom line of triangle.

Cut 2: Side B facing me. Knife Position 2 (pushing knife away from body). Start cut at top with the knife blade straight up, barely inserted into wood. Push knife away from me while gently pushing knife deeper. Gradually lay knife over until blade is again parallel with bottom line of triangle.

Cut 3: Side C facing me. Knife Position 1 (pulling toward body). Start cut at bottom of Cut 1 with the knife blade straight up, barely inserted into wood. Pull knife toward me, gently pushing the knife deeper. Gradually lay knife over to the center. At the center of the cut, gradually straighten and bring the knife out of wood.

Practice carving several individual triangles. When marking your practice board for this exercise, skip a line between each row. This makes the row you are working on easier to see. After a while, instead of turning the board three times for every triangle, you can go down an entire row of triangles with Cut 1. (Photo 22) Then turn the board and do Cut 2 for the row of triangles. (Photo 23)

Turn the board a last time and carve Cut 3 with the same method. (Photo 24) Clean the cuts using the same idea. I do not want you to do this until you are good at carving a single triangle. The reason is that if you carve the entire row with a mistake in your technique, you will be practicing that mistake. You should practice carving a single triangle until you understand the fundamental techniques and can carve one with ease. This way there are no mistakes when you practice carving an entire row of triangles.

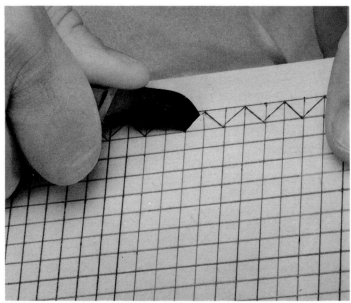

Photo 23: Go back and carve a series of Cut 2.

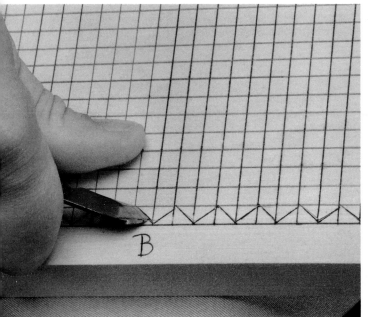

Photo 22: A series of Cut 1.

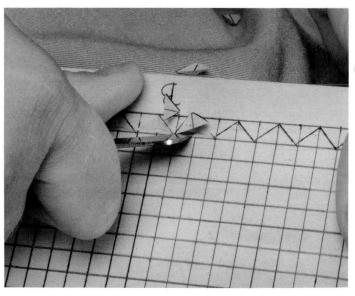

Photo 24: Finally return to do a series of Cut 3.

Stab knife technique

To complete the following projects, you need to learn to use the stab knife. It is very simple. The stab knife does no cutting. It does just what the name implies, stabs. Grasp the knife firmly in your hand just as if you were going to stab something. The longest point of the blade is forward and the back of the blade comes up toward you. I like to put my thumb over the top of the knife. I seem to have more control this way. Line up the point of the knife with the end of the stab mark design. Press down firmly (Photo 25) and rock the knife handle back just a bit (Photo 26). Come back forward and take the knife out of the wood. (Photo 27)

I have designed two projects, a Christmas ornament and a refrigerator magnet. (Photo 28 and Drawings 5 and 6) Carve them after you have practiced Exercise 1.

You will need a circular piece of wood with a 3 inch diameter. It needs to be at least ¼ inch thick. Find and mark the center of the circle. Make perpendicular cross lines in the center of the piece. Trace the design onto the wood. An explanation of this procedure is given on page 52-54. Use the techniques learned in Exercise 1 to carve this design. Finish the stab marks Erase the lines with a pink eraser. Use whatever finish you like to complete the piece. String a green or red ribbon through the hole to hang the ornament. Glue a magnet onto the back for a refrigerator magnet. You have created your first chip carving. Congratulations!

Following are variations on Exercise One. These are borders and designs that can be created by carving only single triangles.

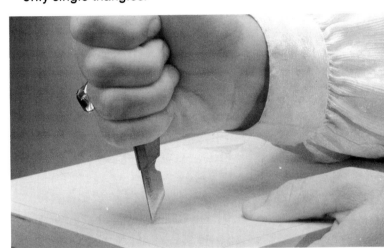

Photo 27: Return the knife back up and take it out.

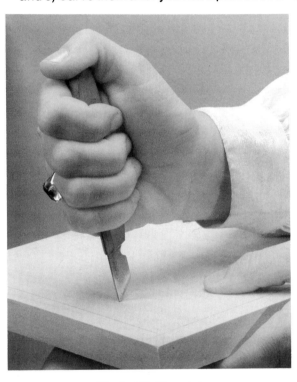

Photo 25: The stab.

Photo 26: Rock it back just a bit.

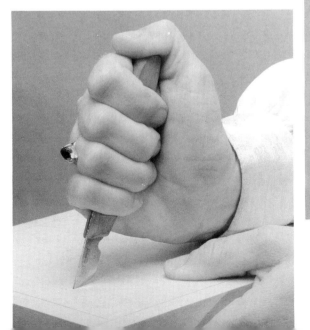

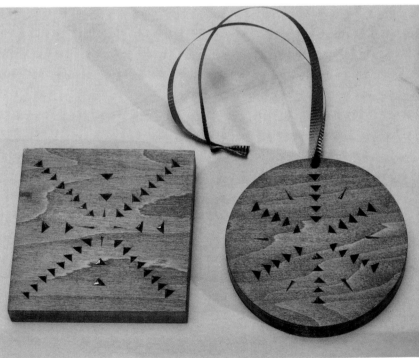

Photo 28: Two projects.

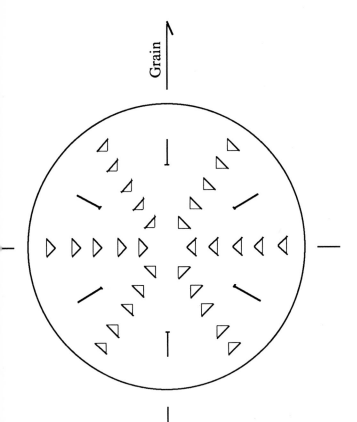

Grain

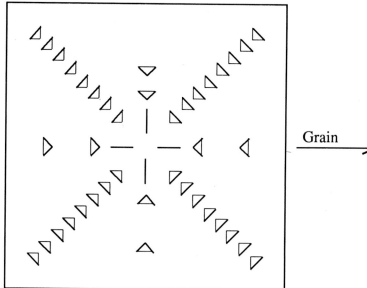

Grain

Drawing 6: The design of the refrigerator magnet.

Drawing 5: The design of the Christmas ornament.

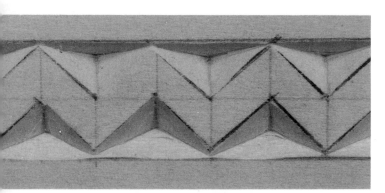

Photo 29: Zig-Zag Border

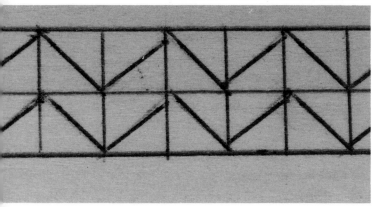

Photo 30: Layout for zig-zag border.

Variation 1: The Zig-Zag Border

A zig-zag border can be created by removing alternate single triangles. (Photo 29) To draw the border on your practice board, just draw two rows of triangles placed identically above and below one another. (Photo 30) By carving away the alternate opposing triangles, the zig-zag effect becomes apparent. To avoid confusion, I suggest that you slightly darken with pencil the triangles to be carved away. (Photo 31) The only difference in carving the lower triangles (the ones facing you), or the higher ones (the ones facing away from you), is the way the board faces. When Side A is facing you, cut the lower triangles using the summary of Cuts 1, 2 and 3 for Exercise 1. (Photo 32)

When the board is turned around to cut the other row of triangles (the top row) Side B will now be facing you. Now the triangles to be cut are toward you. (Photo 33) The sequence and direction of cuts remain the same, but the board directions change. Following is a board direction summary:

Summary of the board direction

Cut 1: Side B facing me, knife Position 1
Cut 2: Side A facing me, knife Position 2
Cut 3: Side D facing me, knife Position 1

This border is effective for particular designs. It is especially adaptable to Southwestern looks, which are always popular.

Photo 31

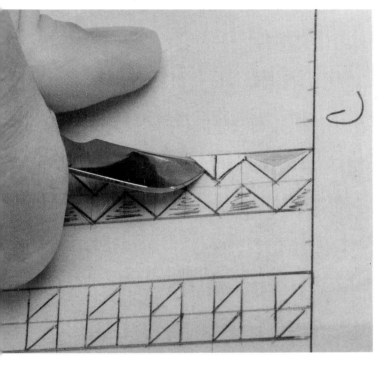

Photo 32: Carving the lower triangles.

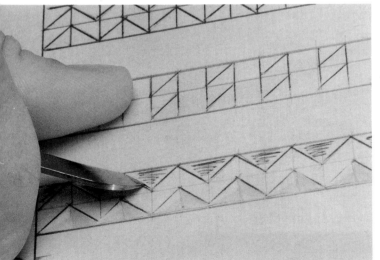

Photo 33: Turn the board and carve the other row.

Variation 2: An Intricate Border Simply Done

This second border, created by removing only single triangles, is one of my favorites. (Photo 34) After removing the triangles, diamond shapes remain. Little simple notches then cut into the diamond shapes give them an intricate look.

This variation and the next one need to be drawn the same. The diamond pattern is drawn on the practice board in much the same way as the single triangle. Use the same ¼ inch grid system. The diamond pattern extends through two lines instead of just one as before. Draw a couple of diamond shapes on the practice board before attempting to draw the entire row. Each diamond will take up four squares (two on top, and two on bottom) of the grid. Begin drawing these diamonds from left to right. Side A should face you for the following explanation. Remember you are now working with two lines of the grid. The first diagonal line extends from the top left hand corner of the first square through the cross lines, and on to the bottom right hand corner. (Photo 35)

Do not skip a square before drawing the next diagonal line as you did when drawing the single triangle layout. The bottom of one diagonal line will be on the same vertical line as the top of the next diagonal line, and so on. Draw all diagonal lines from left to right across one row of your board for top row of diamonds.

Photo 34: A Border

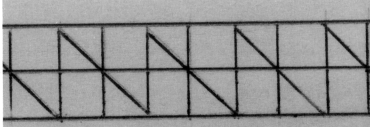

Photo 35: The grid with its diagonal lines for diamonds.

Next, go back and draw the opposing diagonal lines that complete the diamonds. (Photo 36). As a right-handed person, I always like to work from left to right when drawing diagonal lines. I can easily see where I need to put the point of my pencil to slide the ruler over to it. If I work from right to left, the ruler covers the point where I am going. This is awkward and takes more time.

Now that you have drawn a row of diamonds, note the single triangles to be carved away. To avoid confusion at this point, it may be helpful to darken slightly the triangles to be carved out. (Photo 37).

After finishing the preceding steps, the notches need to be marked on the diamonds. When I first started chip carving I could not figure out how to accurately place these notches. Their placement never seemed precisely measured. I realized after carving a few notches that I needed to measure each one. Without measuring and marking them, mine looked crooked and off center. They ruined the clean, sharp look I wanted in my carving. As I stated before, a chip carving is only as good as the pattern drawn on the board.

After years of practice I do not have to measure the notches any more. I can see their placement. This is a skill that develops with practice. There is a simple way to measure these notches using the same method as used to draw the diagonal lines in the first place. Instead of using the same top and bottom points as used for the diamonds, move to the next point (the one between the diamonds). Make a small pencil line to denote each notch (Photo 38). Mark all notches running one way, then go back and mark all the notches running the other way. It won't really take long, and it will help the outcome of your carving tremendously. As I said, after a while it will not be necessary to mark the notches.

Now you are ready to remove the triangles. (Photos 39 and 40) Refer to Variation 1 if you need the guide to help you with board positions. After finishing this step you need to cut the notches into the diamonds. To cut any notch, place the knife so the tip is toward the missing triangle, and the back of the knife is toward the inside of the diamond. Use knife Position 1 for the first cut. Make this cut on the right side of the line. Just make one small, slightly angled push into the wood. (Photo 41) For the second cut use knife Position 2. Make the second cut on the left side of the line. Slightly angle it toward the first cut. (Photo 42) Push gently! The piece should pop out easily. Do this for all remaining notches. Remember, after practicing, do the row of cuts in Position 1 for all the notches running in one direction. Flip the knife to Position 2, go back and do all the cuts to finish the notches on the same side of the diamonds in one row. This technique saves an enormous amount of time. Finish all notches on all diamonds.

This border can compliment almost any design. It is a mainstay in chip carving borders.

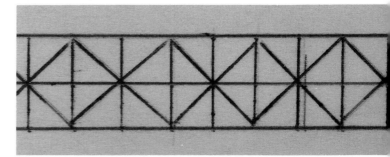

Photo 36: The opposite diagonal creates the diamond.

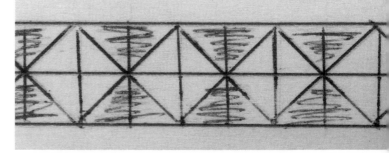

Photo 37: Darken the triangles to be removed.

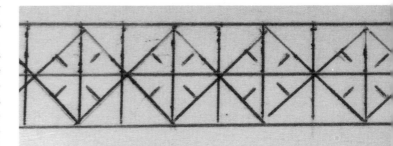

Photo 38: Mark notches on the diamonds

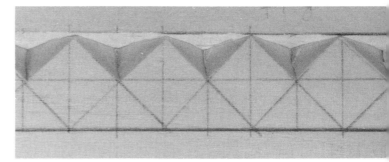

Photo 39

Photo 40

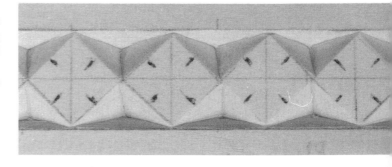

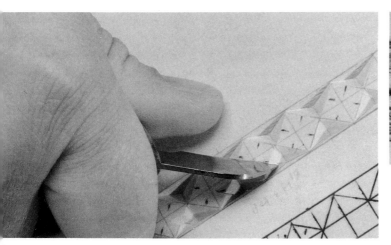

Photo 41: Cut the notches using knife Position 1 in one direction...

Photo 42: and knife Position 2 in the other.

Variation 3

A single triangle again creates the following border. (Photo 43) In this variation the single triangles, placed back to back as in a mirror image, form a diamond shape. The two triangles have one center line in common. As in the preceding variation, carve out the small triangles around the diamond shapes.

Draw this border in the same way as the last variation (Photo 44), except that in this case the area to be removed is not shaded, and the area to remain is. The difference is in the cutting. This diamond will be a negative diamond since it will be carved out. Only the outside edges will be left. After drawing the diamond border on the board, refer to Drawing 7. Before cutting, study the method used to cut the diamond shape. Cut the top triangle exactly like the preceding ones using Cuts 1, 2 and 3. (Photo 45)

Photo 43: A border created by removing only single triangles.

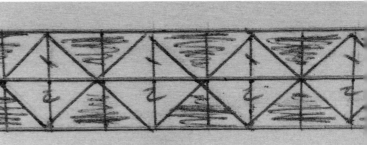

Photo 44: Darkened area: do not remove.

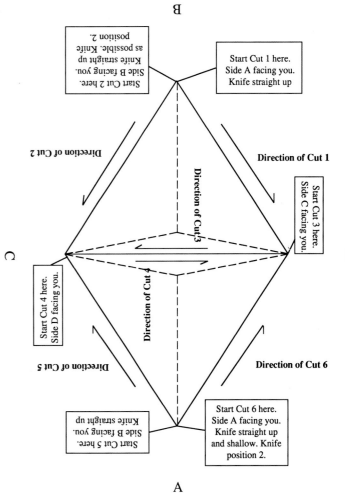

Drawing 7

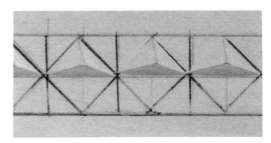

Photo 45: The first triangle carved across the practice board.

Cut 4 is where the new technique begins. Make this cut along the same line as Cut 3, but on the opposite side. You want to leave a single sharp line between the two triangles, but angled down as shown from the top in Drawing 8. By making Cut 4 (the first cut of the second triangle) along this edge, you are decreasing the chances of cutting on through to the first triangle when making Cuts 5 and 6 (the sides).

Consider Cut 4 as a stop cut. Execute Cut 4 with the same technique as Cut 3. (Photos 46 & 47) Remember these are mirror images of each other. Make Cut 5 with the knife in Position 1. (Photo 48) Hold the knife in Position 2 when executing Cut 6, the last cut. (Photo 49) Do this along the row. (Photo 50)

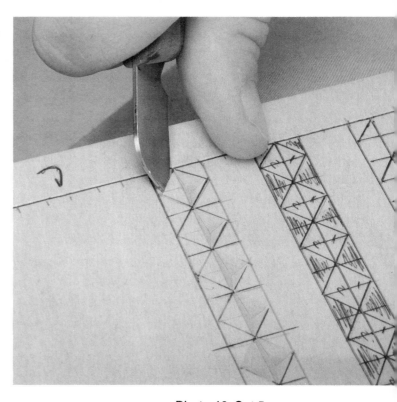

Photo 48: Cut 5

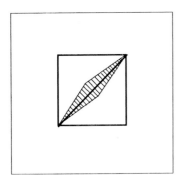

Drawing 8

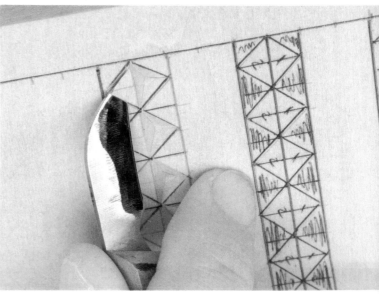

Photo 49: Cut 6

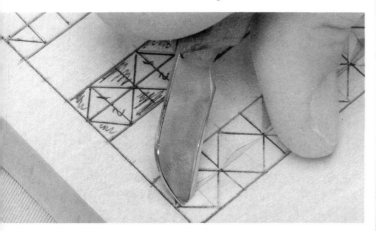

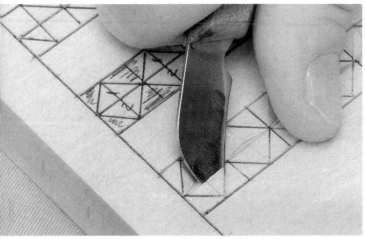

Photos 46 & 47: Cut 4

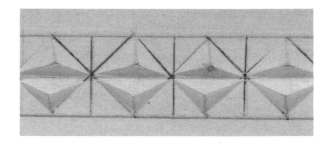

Photo 50

If you need to clean the cuts up, remember to follow the original angles to keep your carving looking clean and sharp.

Carve the small triangles on the edges of the diamonds as two separate rows of triangles. After carving a few diamonds, turn the practice board with Side A facing you. The bottom triangles (between the diamonds), are the ones carved next. These middle triangles are harder to carve because they share a line with the triangles forming the diamonds. You will tend to make more mistakes on these side lines than on the center lines. These diagonal lines will chip out easier than the line in the center of the diamond shape. The center line runs straight with the grain, and the side lines run diagonal across the grain. This part of chip carving is where you become aware of the direction of the grain. Cutting with the grain is much easier, but cutting across the grain will usually cut cleaner. Cutting diagonally across the grain while trying to leave a sharp edge is tricky at first.

A little hint here, do not try too hard. Let up on any unnecessary pressure. Concentrate at the beginning of each cut. It helps me to think at the beginning of each cut that I am not really trying to cut here. (Photos 51, 52, 53) I just pretend I am carving at the beginning of each new side of the triangle. Too much pressure will undercut the other side and pop out a chip that you do not want to pop out. You need to have a feeling of finesse now. Remember chip carving does not need to be deep to be effective. You want shadows, not darkness in your cuts. With practice you will begin to cut clean triangles with sharp edges. You also will develop a "feel" for the depth. I get asked frequently how I keep such an even depth in my carving designs. It was just with practice that my cuts became even.

I know the relationship between the knife, thumb, and the board is the key factor in establishing a consistent depth. Refer to Variation 1 if you need the guide to help you with board positions when carving the triangles in between the diamonds. You should now be practicing to achieve a consistency of look and depth in your carving.

Photo 51

Photo 52

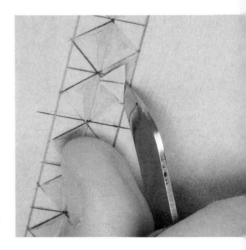

Photo 53

As this book progresses the exercises will become easier for the reader/student to understand and accomplish. We have discussed fundamental techniques such as the way to look at a design, knife positions, and execution procedures. These are the fundamentals for all chip carvings. The following exercises further expand your knowledge based on these fundamental techniques.

Excercise Two

This exercise begins by carving out a single elongated triangle. The single triangle is relatively easy to carve. Next, we progress to two or more adjacent elongated triangles. Following these are designs using the same series of cuts.

Begin by marking the practice board for the single elongated triangles. To do this keep the grain running horizontally as before. Letter the edges. Make a single line around the board, ½ inch from each edge. The triangles measure ½ inch long and ¼ inch wide at the bottom. Therefore, we cannot work from an equal grid as before in Exercise One. The length and width of the triangles are different now.

On the board, with Side A facing you, lay your ruler on the vertical side line. Separate the ½ inch carving rows with ¼ inch spacer rows. If you want to mark off a few rows measure down from the top ½", ¼", ½", ¼", etc. Remember, if your board is square you can make your marks on one line and use the T-square to draw the lines across the board from a single point. If the board is not square enough to do this so the lines are straight, you need to measure down both vertical sides. Use a ruler to draw from one side to the other.

Do not draw all vertical lines yet. Look at the different steps in this exercise. Each one is different vertically from the others. Draw each example vertically as you come to it. If you mark several rows at once, be sure to leave the ¼ inch spacer rows blank. Now your practice board looks like this. (Photo 54)

For the first steps of this exercise the vertical lines need to be ¼ inch apart. Lay your ruler across the top horizontal line and make a small mark at every ¼ inch mark on the ruler. To draw several single elongated triangles you need to make a small mark at the center ·of every other ¼ inch interval on the top horizontal line. These are on the ⅛ inch marks of your ruler. I did not have you mark these before to avoid confusion. It is easier to see the triangle without these lines drawn on the board. (Photo 55)

Some people, with an accurate eye, may not need a ruler for these marks. I can mark them without a ruler now, but I could not when I began to chip carve. Draw the diagonal lines using the small ⅛th inch mark at the top for the center top of the triangle. Be sure to skip a square between the triangles. Remember to mark all diagonal lines running the same way. Then mark the opposite diagonal lines. I cannot stress enough how much time this technique saves. (Photo 56)

Before we cut this triangle let's look ahead. (Drawing 9) Make all the cuts using knife Position 1. You are probably asking yourself, why did we just learn to

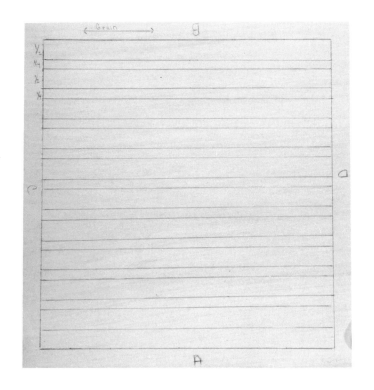

Photo 54: The Practice Board

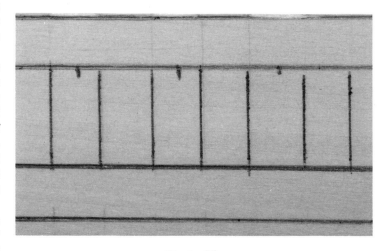

Photo 55

Photo 56

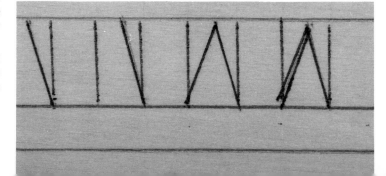

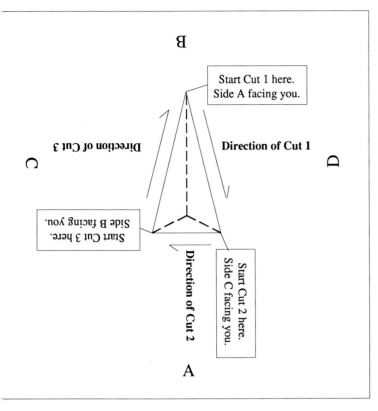

Drawing 9

---

center of the triangle. Your knuckles will be hitting the board.

Make Cut 3 from the bottom of the triangle to the top. At the bottom of the triangle, push the knife into the wood so the point reaches the center. Be sure to lay the knife over so this cut does not get too deep. (Photo 60) Cut toward the top. Gradually straighten the knife and bring the tip out of the wood at the tip of the triangle. Execute the end cut of the triangle with as much finesse as you did the first cut. (Photo 61) Practice the triangles in sequence on the board. (Photo 62)

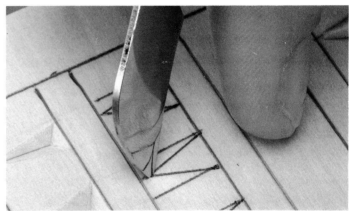

Photo 57: Keep the angle steep.

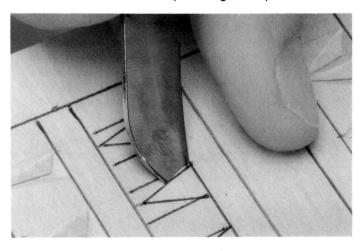

Photo 58

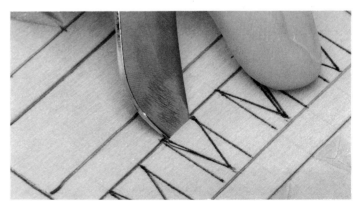

Photo 59

---

carve the single triangle in Exercise One using knife Position 2 for the second cut, yet we are not doing the same here? The answer is, because these triangles are just the first step in learning adjacent triangles. They have a small common point at the top. It is better to end the triangle with the knife coming out at the top, than to begin Cut 2 at the top and carve downward away from your body. The top of these adjacent triangles is a very delicate spot. The carver sees the points of the triangles easier when carving toward their body in Position 1, thus giving them more control here.

Think again about the imaginary center line (denoted by the dotted line on Drawing 9). The top is very narrow. This is a critical point. The knife must be inserted gently into the wood here, at the start of the cut. (Photo 57) When I began to chip carve I remember thinking every time I was about to put my knife into the wood at the top of one of these triangles, "I only need to hint that this is carved." Thinking this helped me greatly. It usually kept me from pushing in too deep at these spots. At the top points, the technique to develop is more finesse than carving.

Execute Cut 1 exactly as we did before in Exercise One. (Photo 58)

Make the second cut straight across the bottom. (Photo 59) Push the knife in and leave it there for the entire cut. **Do not** execute the same as Cut 2 in Exercise One. Lay the knife over so the tip reaches the

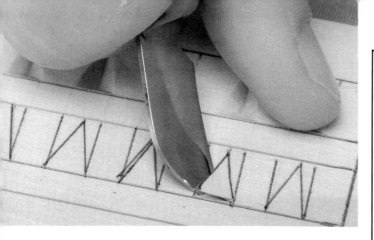

Photo 60

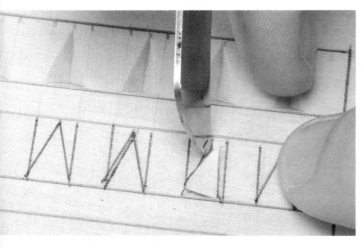

Photo 61

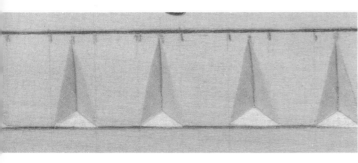

Photo 62: The completed triangles.

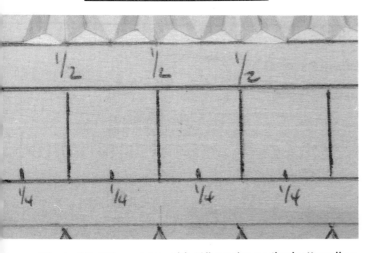

Photo 63: ½" squares with ¼" marks on the bottom line.

Summary of Exercise Two

Following is the summary of the preceding. Again, this works best if you say it to yourself as you are making the cuts.

Knife Position 1 for all cuts.

Cut 1: Side A facing me. Start the cut at the top, with the knife blade straight up and barely inserted into wood. Pull knife toward me, gently pushing deeper and gradually laying the knife over until the blade is parallel with the bottom line of triangle.

Cut 2: Side C facing me. Start the cut at the bottom of the triangle. Push the knife into the wood (laid over) until the point of the knife is at the center of the triangle. Pull the knife toward me using same angle for the entire cut. At line 3 remove the knife from wood.

Cut 3: Side B facing me. Start the cut at the bottom of the triangle. Push the knife into the wood (laid over) until the point of the knife is at the center of the triangle. Pull knife toward me, straightening and coming out of the wood as I go. Near the top bring the knife out of the wood, barely carving the tip.

Practice carving several elongated triangles before moving to the next step.

Variation 1: Adjacent Elongated Triangles

To draw adjacent triangles on the practice board again use ½ inch horizontal lines. These triangles have a pyramid look. They are much wider at the bottom than at the top. Lay your ruler across the horizontal line that marks the top of the triangles. Make small marks on this line at ½ inch intervals. Move your ruler to the next line down, the line that will be at the bottom of the triangles. Mark this line with small marks at ¼ intervals. Draw vertical lines down from the ½ inch marks. These lines are the center of the pyramids. (Photo 63)

Draw the diagonal lines from the ¼ inch marks to the center top. (Photo 64).

Cut the adjacent triangles with the same technique as Exercise 2, Step 1. As you do a series of cuts always have the carved part behind your hand. The part that is to be carved is in front of your hand. A right-handed person will always start a series of cuts from the right. A left-handed person will start from the left. Always work toward what needs carved. My explanations are for the right handed person since I am right handed.

Cuts 1, 2, and 3 are the same as Cuts 4, 5, and 6. (Drawing 10) Make Cut 4, or the first cut down the second triangle, on the same line as Cut 3. There is no real trick I can tell you for carving this common line. (Photo 65)

You will mess up here at first. It does get a little more difficult. It will not take long to accomplish this exercise if you stay with it. Follow the summary, practice the technique and you will do fine.

Use the summary for Cuts 1, 2, and 3 over for all the cuts. Instead of Cuts 1, 2, 3, 4, 5, and 6,—they are 1, 2, 3, 1, 2, and 3. The sequence is down the right side, across

Photo 64

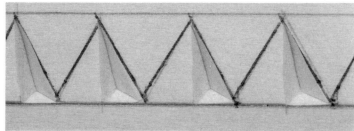

Photo 65

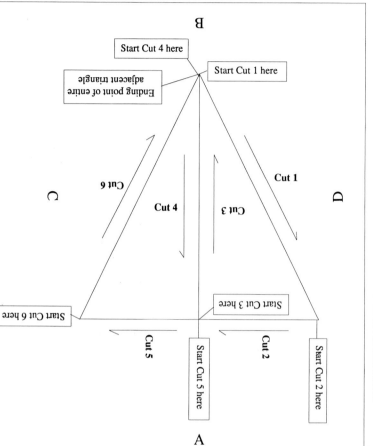

Drawing 10

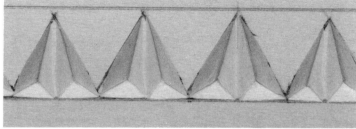

Photo 66: The complete triangle.

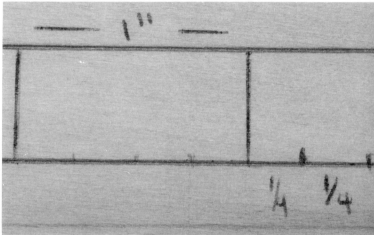

Photo 67: With horizontal lines ½″ apart, mark 1″ vertical lines. Divide the bottom line into ¼″ segments.

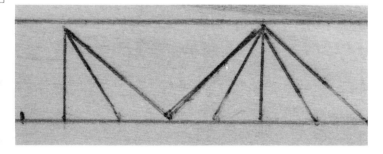

Photo 68: From the upper end of the vertical line draw lines to the ¼″ marks.

the bottom, and back up the left side. Down—Across—Up. (Photo 66)

In this exercise you learn to meet adjacent triangles at the top without popping out the wrong chips, and to leave a single line between triangles. These are two key techniques that must be practiced. It is essential to learn these to become a proficent chip carver. The designs using these techniques are endless.

Variation 2

In this variation I just want you to keep fanning the triangles out at the bottom. Execute the cuts in the same way as before. Start from the right and think; down—across—up.

Now it gets fun! (Photos 67, 68, 69)

Photo 69: Start from the right and carve each adjacent triangle in the way described: down across up.

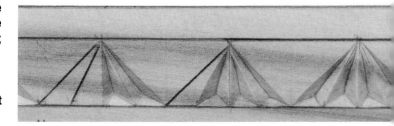

Exercise Three

Photo 70

Photo 71

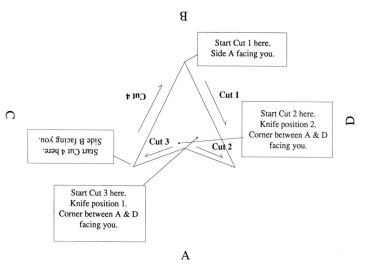

Drawing 11

Photo 72

This is a new technique, used in carving Designs 4 and 5, (Photo 70).

Draw an elongated triangle as you did in Exercise Two, Step 1. Measure up from the center bottom ⅛ inch and draw the inner triangle. To draw an entire row of these triangles draw a line parallel with the bottom line. Place a small mark at the center of the triangle along this line. Draw the small triangle as shown. By placing a small triangle at the bottom of the large triangle, the number of cuts increases from three to four. Refer to the diagram. (Drawing 11).

Start Cut 1 at the top as always. (Photo 71) At the end of the cut you need to straighten the knife back up so as not to undercut the triangle at the bottom.

Execute Cut 2 with the knife held in Position 2. Look at the diagram (Drawing 11) to see where to start this cut. Start the cut ahead of the top point of the small triangle. Follow the direction of the side of the small triangle. Starting the cut early insures that a sharp point remains. Push the knife in at the beginning of the cut. Execute the cut. (Photo 72)

Use knife Position 1 again for Cut 3. Start this cut ahead of the top point of the triangle. Follow down the side of the triangle. Push the knife in at the beginning of the cut. Execute Cut 3. (Photo 73) The Cuts 2 and 3 cross above the bottom triangle.

Make Cut 4 using knife Position 1. Start at the bottom of the triangle with the knife barely inserted into the wood. Cut from the bottom to the top. Lay your knife over in the middle of the cut, and straighten again at the top. (Photo 74)

Photo 73

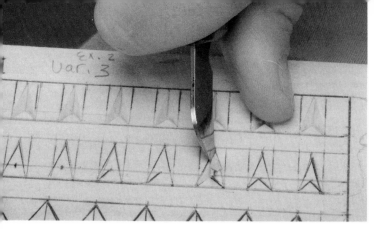

Photo 74

Summary of Exercise Three

Cut 1: Side A facing me. In knife Position 1 start the cut at the top. Begin with the knife blade straight up and barely inserted into wood. Pull the knife toward me, gently pushing the knife deeper and gradually laying the knife over to center. At the center, gradually straighten and bring the knife out of the wood at the bottom of triangle.

Cut 2: Corner of Sides A and C facing me. In knife Position 2 start the cut a little above the bottom triangle. Push the knife in following down the side line of the triangle.

Cut 3: Corner of Sides A and D facing me. With knife Position 1 start the cut a little above the bottom triangle. Push the knife in, following down the side of the triangle.

Cut 4: Side B facing me, knife Position 1. Start the cut at the bottom of triangle with the knife blade barely inserted into wood. Pull the knife toward me, gently pushing the knife deeper and gradually laying it over to the middle of the triangle. At the middle, gradually straighten and bring knife out of the wood at the point.

Practice this technique on single and adjacent triangles. There are many designs that use this technique. (Photo 76)

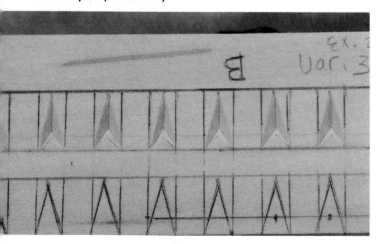

Photo 75: Finished

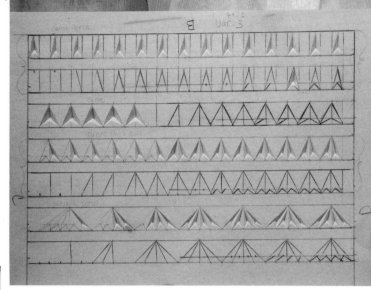

Photo 76: A practice board.

DESIGNS AND APPLICATION

Let's work on a few designs that use the techniques in Exercise Three. Instead of calling the following "steps," I want to call them "designs." You are no longer learning just technique. You are now learning how to apply those techniques to create beautiful designs.

As far as putting these patterns on the board, I am approaching some of these designs in two ways. I have talked to many people about what they wanted in a chip carving book. Some wanted to learn to draw the designs, others did not. For this reason I have included several designs here that can be traced onto the board. They can be reduced or enlarged at a copy machine to fit onto any project. I have also shown how to draw some as well, for those that want to learn. Designs 1, 3, and 4 need to be measured. Trace Design 2 onto the board. You have an option to draw or trace Designs 5 and 6. I have also included more designs that apply to this exercise, which need no discussion because they employ the same techniques.

Designs 1, 3, 4, and 5 are basically 1 inch square, divided into four half-inch blocks. To create these squares, lay out your practice board with horizontal lines measuring down ½"—½" - ¼" (the quarter inch is a spacer row), repeated the length of the board. All the vertical lines are ½" apart.

DESIGN 1 (Photo 80)

You will need a small protractor to draw Design 1. Think of this design as one square inch. On the board four equal sections divide the one square inch. Position the protractor where it hits both the middle top and side bottom of the square. (Photo 77).

Draw the arcs for both sides. Always draw design lines onto the board as lightly as possible. To draw the lines that radiate up from the center place your ruler on a vertical side line. Put ¼ inch marks between the ½ inch lines. Draw horizontal lines across the board at these ¼" marks. (Photo 78)

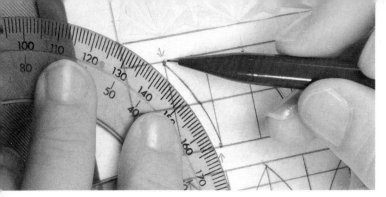

Photo 77

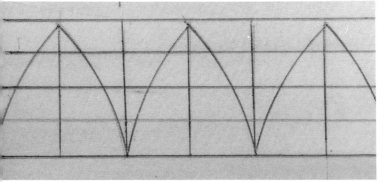

Photo 78

I am not summarizing each cut. If you do the cuts in the proper sequence, you automatically hold the board correctly. Just think; down across up. (Drawing 12)

Remember to barely cut the points. Each point does not have to go completely to the end to look right in the completed design. If you get to triangle 4, for instance, and you do not have enough room to cut to the very end, go ahead and make the triangle just a little short of the end. This gives the next point a little more room and everything looks fine in the end. I used to go crazy trying to make these points meet perfectly every time. One day I discovered that I could do this, and executing the meeting of these points became much easier. Now carve Design 1. Have fun doing it.

If you would like to make a border out of these fans, simply draw a ¼ inch equilateral triangle between them as shown. Carve it as two adjacent triangles. You can even go one step further and put stab marks below these triangles. This creates a very effective and unique border. (Photo 80)

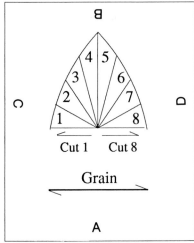

Drawing 12

Draw the lines from the bottom center up and out to the point where the ¼″ lines intersect with the arcs. Draw the lines lightly with the pencil. (Photo 79)

Remember I am explaining the sequence of cuts as a right handed person. The left handed person would carve in the opposite direction.

To begin the sequence, Side C should face you. Begin and end each cut at the bottom center of this design. It is just a series of adjacent triangles. Turn the board in smaller increments now. Hold the board so that you look straight on at the triangle you are carving.

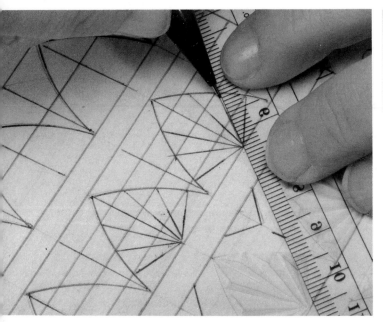

Photo 79

Photo 80: Border using Design 1.

DESIGN 2

This design is an extension of Design 2. I have made a pattern for this design. (Drawing 13).

This pattern only has the points marked that the lines radiating from the center connect to. This keeps the drawing precise. To put the design onto the board, first trace the design onto a piece of parchment paper. Refer to page 54 for instructions on this process. With Side A facing you, draw a horizontal line across the board at least 1¾ inches below the last line. This line should be parallel with the grain. Be sure to mark center and the points around the oval on this particular drawing. Draw the radiating lines by connecting the dots. Be sure each line crosses through the center.

Begin to carve this as you did the preceding design. (Drawing 14).

Cut 1 is in the middle of the oval. I like to begin and end a series of triangles with the grain. It makes the last cut easier. The grain is running horizontally on the practice board when Side A faces you. If you were carving a project in which the grain ran vertically, you would begin the series by cutting the triangles that run up and down, or parallel with the grain. For now, on our practice board, execute the series as shown. (Photo 81) This design is simple, yet elegant.

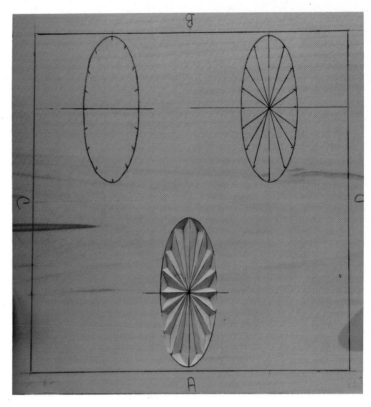

Photo 81

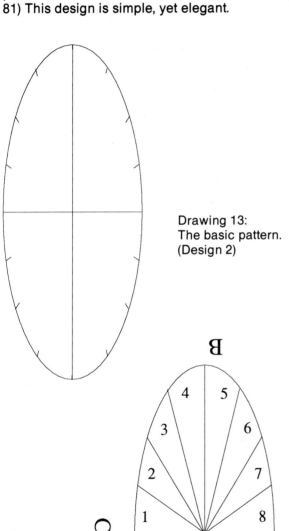

Drawing 13:
The basic pattern.
(Design 2)

Drawing 14:
The cut sequence.

Grain

A

DESIGN 3

This is a very traditional design. This is only one square out of a repeating pattern called a grid. (Photo 82)

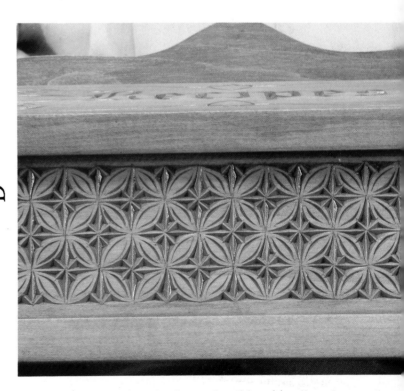

Photo 82: A recipe box using this grid pattern

Photo 83

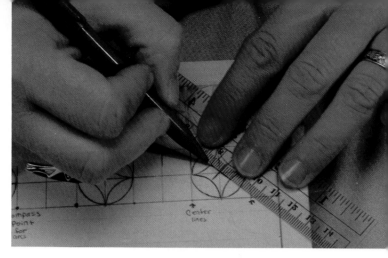

Photo 85

Photo 84

I numbered the sequence of cuts for each corner triangle for you. (Drawing 15) The easiest way to cut the corner triangles is to go all the way down each line, then go back and cut the curve side of each triangle. It looks straighter if you do this, and saves time. A study of carving triangles with a curved edge follows later in this book.

To finish this design there are small lines carved into the solid ovals. Carve these using knife Position 1. Make the first cut toward you, along the right side of the line. Then turn the board the opposite direction and make the cut on the other side of the line. I discuss carving single and straight lines more in the last exercise. (Photo 86)

This design, again, measures one square inch. Draw the horizontal and vertical lines the same as in Design 1. You now have one square inch divided into four equal sections. Next, put the point of your compass on the center of the square inch. (Photo 83)

Adjust the compass so that it barely touches the sides of the square. Draw a circle. With the compass in the same adjustment, move the point to a corner of the square. (Photo 84)

Draw a portion of a circle inside the original large circle. Do the same from each corner. If you were drawing a grid, each circle drawn from a corner would overlap another square. To draw the diagonal lines, simply lay a ruler from corner to corner and draw the line. (Photo 85)

Carve the design by using the same cutting sequence as in the oval design. Cut the corner triangles around the circle using only knife Position 1. In a grid design these are adjacent triangles. When cutting these triangles I try to make the first cut with the grain. Then follow around each triangle. The last cut is cross-grain whenever possible. As a general rule, a chip pops out easier if the last cut is cross-grain. One cannot always make the last cut cross-grain because of the lay of the design. When looking at how to carve a particular section, I try to follow that rule whenever possible.

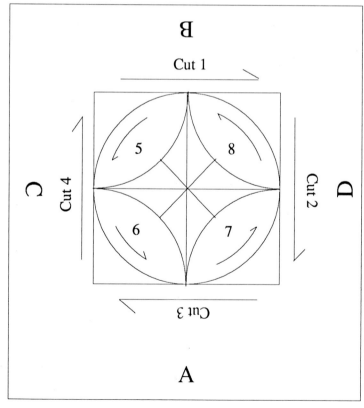

Drawing 15

Photo 86

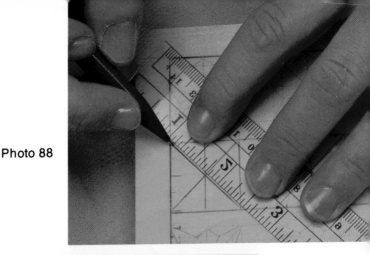

Photo 88

DESIGN 4

Here are the drawings for the next two designs, if you wish to trace them (Drawings 16 & 17) Refer again to the tracing instructions if you need them. (Photo 87).

Following is the procedure for drawing these designs for those who wish to learn. Begin to draw this design by laying out the square inches on your board. Side A is still facing you. Draw diagonal lines from corner to corner. (Photo 88)

Next lay a ruler on a horizontal line and make a mark ⅛th inch from each side. (Photo 89)

Connect these marks with vertical lines. Use either a T-square or a speed square to draw these lines onto the pattern (Photo 90). If the board is not square you need to mark both sides and use a ruler.

After you have the ⅛ inch lines on the diagram, mark the center of each segment. (Photo 91) Draw the diagonal lines to complete the triangles. (Photo 92) The sequence of drawing is shown in Photo 93.

Carve this design by realizing that it is a series of adjacent triangles. Use the technique explained in Exercise Three to carve each of these triangles. (Photo 94)

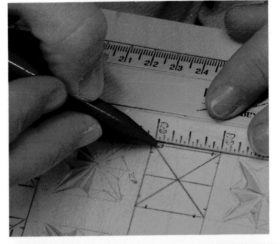

Photo 89

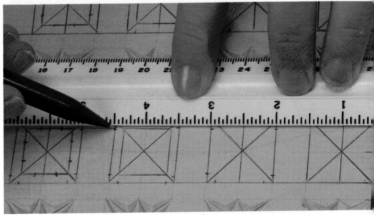

Photo 90

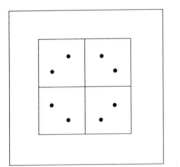 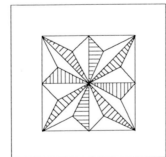

Drawings 16 (pattern) and 17 (finished)

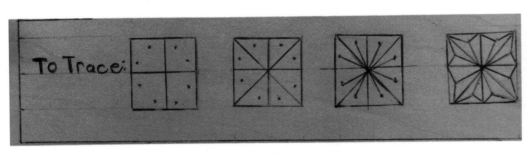

Photo 87

Photo 91

Photo 92

Photo 96: The carving (Design 5)

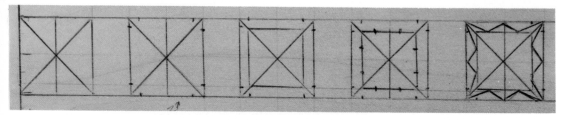

Photo 93: The sequence of drawing.

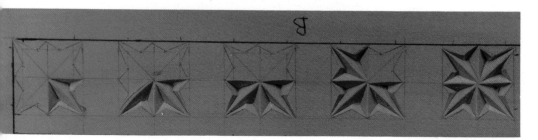

Photo 94: The carving sequence (Design 4)

Design 5

Design 5 is the same as Design 4 with four more diagonal lines added. (Photo 93, 95) Use the center point of the inside triangles to connect the lines. Carve this design using the adjacent triangle technique. (Photo 96) Exercise Three does not apply to this design. Carve it using the same three basic down-across-up cuts.

This completes the section on carving adjacent triangles. Following are different designs created with the techniques already shown in this book. (Photo 97; Drawings 18-24) These would make good designs for almost any project.

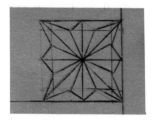

Photo 95: The pattern

Photo 97: Designs using these basic techniques.

Drawing 18 & 19

Drawing 22 & 23

Drawing 20 & 21

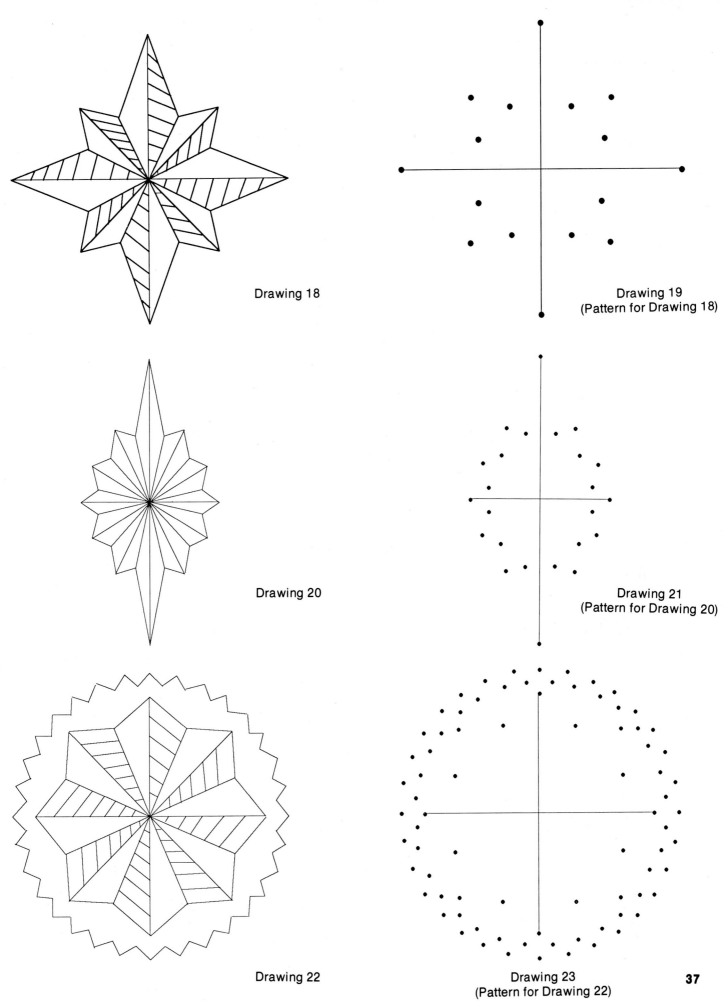

Drawing 18

Drawing 19
(Pattern for Drawing 18)

Drawing 20

Drawing 21
(Pattern for Drawing 20)

Drawing 22

Drawing 23
(Pattern for Drawing 22)

Exercise Four
Single and Adjacent Curved Triangles

The next two exercises analyze the technique for carving curved chips. Exercise Four studies carving both the single and the adjacent curved triangles. This is the natural progression from adjacent straight triangles. Many of the same techniques apply to the next exercises. Exercise Five studies carving an oval. The designs using curved and oval chips are closely bound to one another.

For Exercise Four the practice board is laid out for you. The design is so that you can trace the examples onto your practice board. This exercise follows an ordered sequence. (Drawing 25)

On the practice board draw line for the ½ inch border. Letter the edges, making sure the grain is on a horizontal plane in front of you. Trace this exercise onto the board. A short cut is just to trace all the examples that go the same direction (i.e. 1A, 2A, 3A, etc.), and copy them onto the board. Then remove the parchment paper, flip it over, move it down one row on the board, and trace it over again. Flipping over the parchment paper gives you the same design, backward. It saves tracing time.

Notice that the first triangle in each of the first four rows has the dotted center lines marked. I suggest that you trace this one as is on to your practice board, and then leave it uncarved. This way you have a reference point to look at while carving the rest of the row.

Cut these examples using knife Position 1.

Variation 1

Look at the enlarged triangle (Drawing 26). Note how far the center dotted line is from the curved edge, and how close it is to the straight edge. Remember, this is the bottom of the cut. It is where the point of the knife needs to be. Notice how far the knife needs to be laid over while executing the curved cut. For greater ease of explanation and understanding, Drawing 26 is meant to show how to handle the depth of the knife. I have not numbered the cuts because they differ depending on the direction that the triangle faces. There are separate drawings to show the direction of cuts. The depth, however does not change. Because it is still the same triangle, with the same angles no matter which way it faces. At this point in the book the diagrams (Drawings 27 & 28) are really self explanatory.

For these triangles the rules are; always cut from right to left (for the right handed person), and always make the first cut with the grain. Practice carving these triangles using the diagrams. (Photos 99-106)

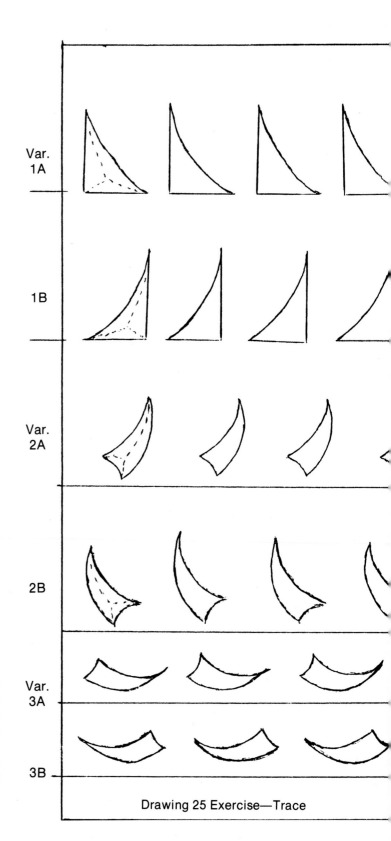

Var. 1A

1B

Var. 2A

2B

Var. 3A

3B

Drawing 25 Exercise—Trace

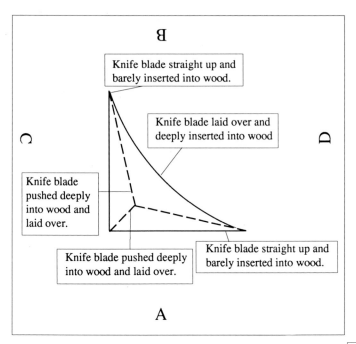

Drawing 26

B

Knife blade straight up and barely inserted into wood.

Knife blade laid over and deeply inserted into wood

C

D

Knife blade pushed deeply into wood and laid over.

Knife blade pushed deeply into wood and laid over.

Knife blade straight up and barely inserted into wood.

A

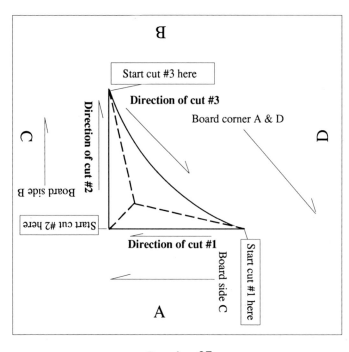

Drawing 27

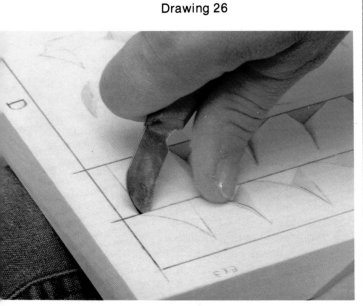

Photo 99: The beginning of cut 1

Photo 100: The end of cut 1

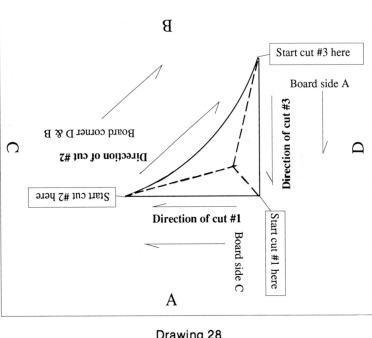

Drawing 28

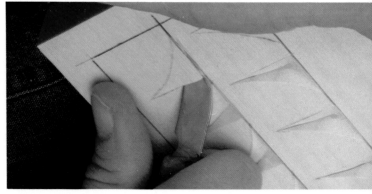

Photo 101: The beginning of cut 2

Photo 102: The end of cut 2

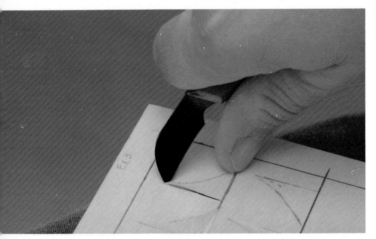

Photo 103: The beginning of cut 3

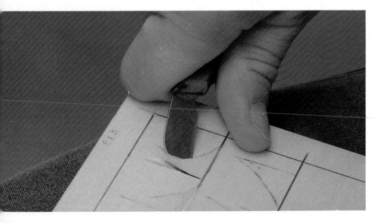

Photo 104: The middle of the curved cut

Photo 105: The end of the curved cut

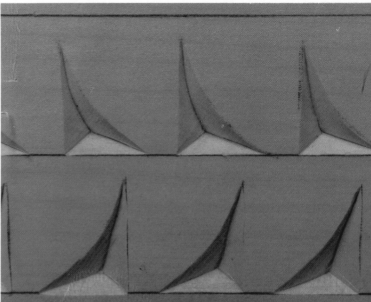

Photo 106: The results

Variation 2

These are basic single triangular chips. They are a major underlying element in many chip carving designs. Execute these using the same down—across —up technique as used in the previous exercise. These are usually adjacent triangles also.

The enlarged drawings (Drawings 29 & 30) for this example show the starting point and direction of each cut. The same rule of carving from right to left applies to these triangles. Cut Variation 2 from right to left no matter if it is the convex (curving outward) or concave (curving inward) side of the triangle. What matters, is working from the direction of whatever hand you are using. Right-handed people work from right to left. Left-handed people work from left to right. Remember most of the explanations in this book are for right-handed people.

The importance of this exercise is to get the feeling of rolling the knife as you execute each cut. I purposely curved the bottom of these triangles so that you could practice that feeling on all sides. I enjoy the feeling of carving these more than any other shape in chip carving. They are fun to carve.

The dotted lines again indicate the depth of the knife. Cut 1 (Photo 107) starts with the knife straight up and inserted gently into the wood. Lay the knife over and push deeper as you execute the cut. End with the knife laid over so that your knuckles are touching the board, and the blade inserted deeply into the wood (Photo 108).

The beginning of Cut 2 (Photo 109), for both the concave and convex triangles, differs a little from anything we studied so far. I can only explain this by the "feeling" I have when I carve it. I cannot say to either insert the knife gently, or push in deeply to begin this cut. It is more a combination of both. You want to insert gently, roll, and push, all at once. It is all one motion here. You end with the knife laid over and inserted deeply. (Photo 110)

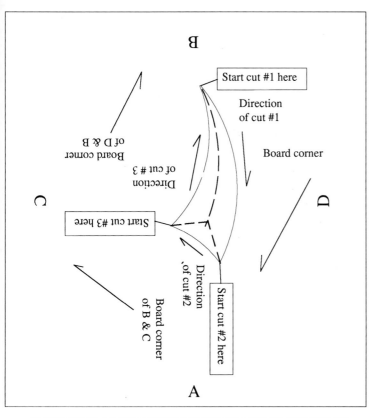

B

Start cut #1 here

Direction
of cut #1

Board corner

Board corner
of D & B

Direction
of cut # 3

C

Start cut #3 here

D

Direction
of cut #2

Start cut #2 here

Board corner
of B & C

A

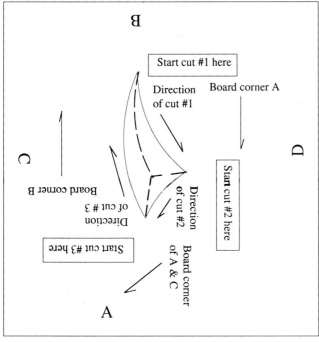

B

Start cut #1 here

Direction
of cut #1

Board corner A

C

Board corner B

D

Start cut #2 here

Direction
of cut #2

Direction
of cut # 3

Start cut #3 here

Board corner
of A & C

A

Drawings 29 & 30

Photo 107

Photo 108

Photo 109

Photo 110

To start Cut 3 (Photo 111) lay the knife over so that your knuckles are on the board, and really push the knife into the wood. Straighten, and begin to pull the blade out of the wood as you execute this cut (Photo 112). Practice Variation 2 using the diagrams. (Photos 113, 114, 115)

41

Photo 111

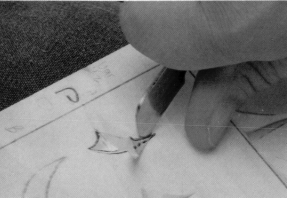

Photo 112

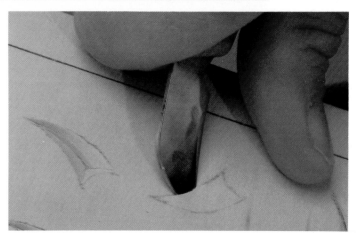

Photo 113: For the right-handed person the carving proceeds from right to left, but it does not matter if the right side is concave or convex. Here Cut 1 is on the concave side.

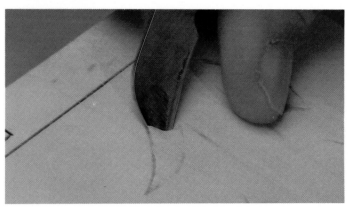

Photo 114: Cut 2 is on the short side.

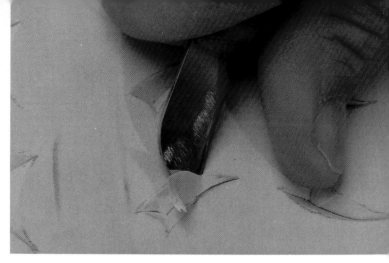

Photo 115: Cut 3 is along the convex side.

Variation 3

The reason I put Variation 3 in this exercise is to show you how to work with the grain here. Note the way this triangle almost runs with the grain, but not quite. For an instant you are almost cutting with the grain. Think of it as cutting into, with, and out of the grain. This makes carving the curved part of the triangle difficult. The grain wants to take you with it here. Sometimes these cuts become jagged. Carvers call this chatter. To avoid chattering around a curve, sometimes you have to hold the knife straight and cut the fibers at the surface of the wood. (Photo 116) Do not cut deeply. Only cut the surface fibers. Then go back and make the cut deeper with the proper depth. (Photo 117) This usually stops the wood from chattering. Another technique is to let up on the pressure at the point where the grain runs into the side of the triangle. Yet, you must control the knife in these spots. Do not let the grain control your knife. I know this is a feeling that comes with practice. You cannot use too much pressure, but you need to control the knife. Practice is the only way to acquire this technique. Carve these triangles using the same cuts as in Variation 2. (Photos 118, 119, 120)

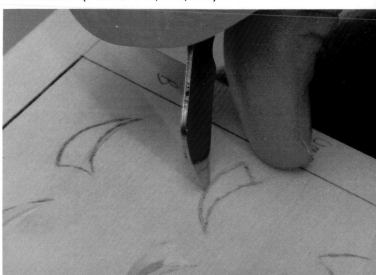

Photo 116: Cutting surface fibers.

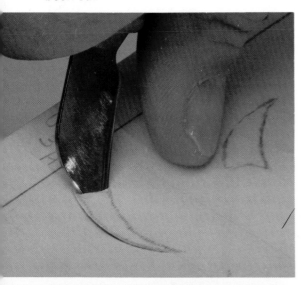

Photo 117: Cutting deeper after the surface fibers have been cut.

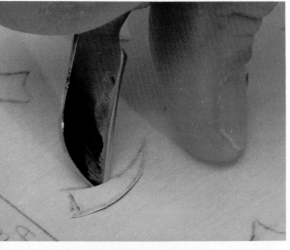

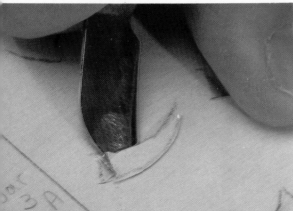

Variation 4

Variation 4 works on adjacent curved triangles. (Drawing 31) Carve these triangles by repeating Cuts 1, 2, and 3. Follow the basic rules; carve from right to left and gently insert the knife at the points. Remember to use finesse. If you have trouble with the last cut because of the grain, cut the top fibers first, and let up on the pressure.

Variation 4B is the most difficult. It is hard **not** to insert the blade too deeply into the point. It is because of the physical aspects of the way you have to hold the knife, and the direction of the first cut (Photo 121). The knife wants to go in further than it should. If it does, it undercuts the line of the next triangle. Be careful at this point. Concentrate when starting each cut (Photo 122). Make the final cut with as much care as the first cut (Photo 123). One also can undercut the center line at this point in the cut. Practice Variation 4 using the techniques and diagrams from Variation 2.

Var.
4A

Photo 118

4B

4A
extended

Photo 119

4B
extended

Photo 120

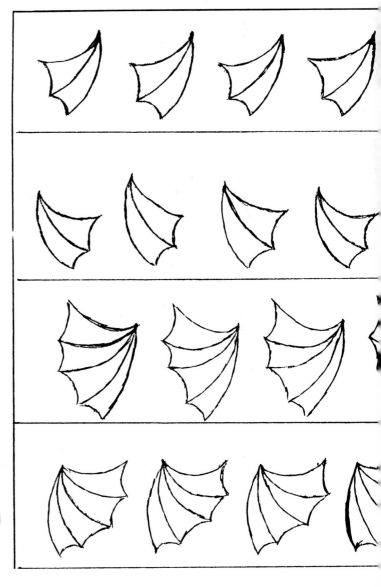

Drawing 31

43

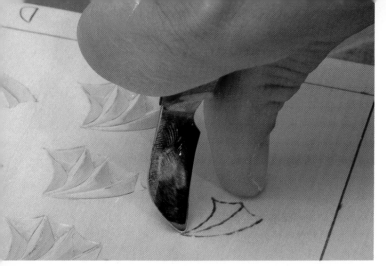

Photo 121

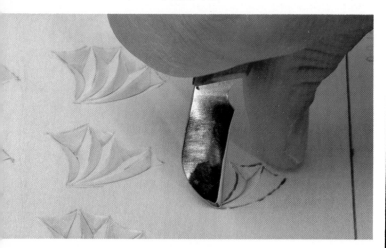

Photo 122

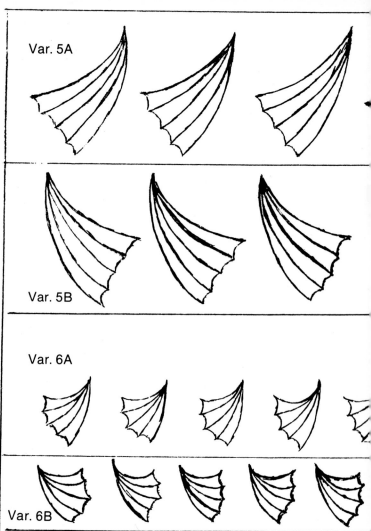

Var. 5A

Var. 5B

Var. 6A

Var. 6B

Drawing 32

Variation 6

This variation is a study in finesse. It will hone the skill of making small cuts. Execute each cut with a very light touch. It is easy to undercut the lines forming the adjacent triangles, thus popping out the wrong chips. Concentrate with every cut. Execute with the same techniques. Remember concentrate, and carve lightly.

This concludes this exercise. Next is a very short study of cutting an oval.

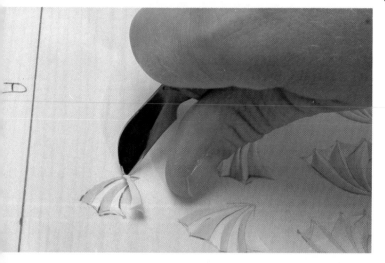

Photo 123

Variation 5

These are examples of elongated, curved, adjacent triangles. (Drawing 32) One needs to practice these shapes before encountering them in a design. Because the technique is the same as the last example, there are no diagrams or explanations. Note, the triangles are thinner, so you do not need to push the knife in as far. It requires a lighter, easier touch.

Exercise Five
The Oval

Two simple cuts make up the basic oval. (Drawing 33) The easiest way to practice carving it is with the basic six sided rosette. (Drawing 34) Follow the direction found on page 55 to draw the rosette.

Carve the oval using knife Position 1. Start carving on any oval. Use the same basic techniques as with the other shapes in this book. Make the first cut on the right side of the oval (Photo 124). Notice how close the ovals are at the center of the design. Insert the knife gently to avoid popping out the center. Lay the knife over in the middle of the cut (Photo 125), then straighten and bring the knife out of the wood to end the cut (Photo 126). Turn the board in the opposite direction and execute the second cut exactly like the first one (Photo 127). Carve all the ovals. (Photo 128)

Photo 124

Photo 125

Photo 126

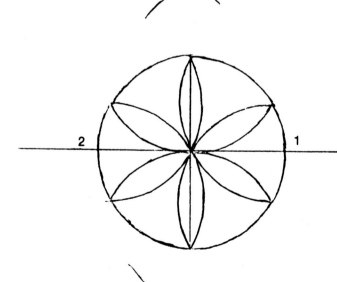

Drawing 33

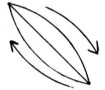

Drawing 34

Photo 127

Photo 130

Photo 133

Photo 128

Photo 131

Photo 134

Photo 129

Photo 132

Photo 135

Frequently in designs, the oval has a diamond placed in the center of it. This increases the difficulty. Follow the directions with the diagram on page 55 (Drawing 42) to draw this design on the board. Execute this carving using the same procedure as in Exercise Three. Do not use the part of the summary that tells the side of the board that should face you. The basic technique is the same. Cut the length of each side with one cut. (Photos 129-130) These are the first two cuts. Cut down the right side, and then back up the left side. The knife needs to be straight and almost taken out of the wood at the center, around the diamond. Photos 131-134 show the succession and knife positions for the rest of the cuts. Practice carving these ovals (Photo 135).

Exercise Six
Single Straight Lines

Straight lines, basically used to border projects, can stand alone (Photo 136), or be on both sides of a carved border (Photo 137). They are also used in some grids (Photo 138). Straight lines that run with the grain are more difficult to carve than lines running across the grain. Grain is never perfectly straight. The irregularities in the grain want to pull the knife with them, making the knife stray from the straight line. Do not get discouraged if your first lines are wavy and jagged. This is a skill that only comes with much practice.

When I began carving straight lines I thought they were impossible. This is when I derived what I call a "trick," which made carving straight lines much easier. Draw the straight line where you want it on the board with the mechanical pencil. Make sure the line is where you want it. Next, go over that line with a dull pencil, using a ruler to guide you. Make the line very heavy. When you do this, be sure to give the dull lead a little extra room with the ruler. This lead will take up more space than the mechanical pencil lead. This heavy line gives you the appearance of having two sides to carve, instead of trying to carve down one thin line. It also indents the wood a little and gives the knife blade a track to follow. By doing this the knife will not stray as much when cutting with the grain. I used this "trick" for a long time. (Photo 139) Now I can carve a thin straight line with ease.

Photo 137: Parallel lines on each side of a border.

Photo 138: Grid of single lines

Photo 136: Single line border

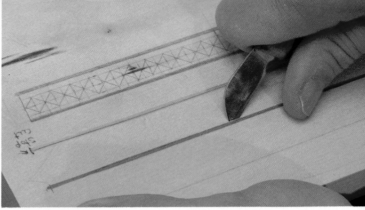

Photo 141

Photo 139

Draw a straight line on your practice board. Before carving the line, make a stop cut with your knife at each end of the line. A stop cut is just a little slice in the wood (Photo 140). Just stick the point of the knife into the wood at the end of the line, and bring it back out again. Its purpose is to stop the knife and the line at the end of the cut. Always make stop cuts at the end of a straight line.

Carve a line with two cuts, both in knife Position 1. Start the first cut on the right side of the line, at the end farthest away from your body. Pull the knife down the line, toward your body (Photo 141). Lay the knife over, but not so far that your knuckles touch the board. Turn the board and cut at the same angle down the other side of the line (Photo 142). The cut looks like this when finished (Drawing 36). The cut should not be too deep or too shallow. Be sure your thumb is on the board, as it should always be.

Try to look ahead of the knife while carving a straight line. I also try to look for any irregularities in the grain. I know I have to use a little extra grit at these spots to make the knife do what I want it to do, instead of straying with the grain.

Do not try too hard when carving straight lines. By that I mean do not use too much pressure and strength. They are easiest when you just let them happen. Using too much pressure also causes the knife to undercut the other side of the line. Turn the board around and carve down the second side. This skill does require practice.

Photo 142

Drawing 36

When carving a straight line around a border, make the first cut away from the border (Photo 143). The space between the line and the border is usually narrow. It is easy for the point of the knife to reach the edge of the border and pop out chips along this edge. Making the first cut away from the border stops this from happening.

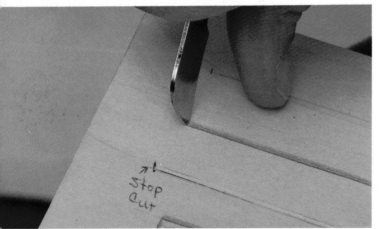

Photo 140: Stop cuts.

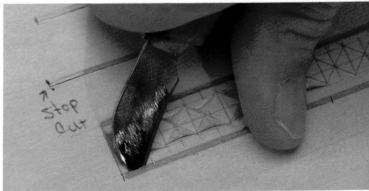

Photo 143

Exercise Seven
Curved Single Lines

I must be honest with you, curved lines are probably the hardest cuts to execute cleanly in chip carving. It is because a curved line runs in and out of the grain. Look at the diagram of the complete circle (Drawing 37), and note how the grain runs into it. The sides of this circle run cross grain. The top of the circle runs parallel with the grain for an instant. When the knife gets to this point the grain does not want to let it go. The grain keeps pulling the knife straight here.

Because of the grain, the wood wants to chatter around these cuts. Practice carving a complete circle. To do this I suggest that you use the same idea as the dull lead trick. Only, for the circle draw two circles very close to each other. Make the first circle with your compass, then lessen the adjustment, just a tiny bit, and draw a second circle. This gives you two sides to carve, instead of one thin line. I like to use a circle around my rosettes on some of my simpler pieces. I have my system of carving single line circles.

I used to applique on a sewing machine. If you are not familiar with this, it is basically zig-zagging a piece of material, cut in a design, onto a larger project. To make the applique smooth and rich looking, the zig-zags are close to one another with no spaces between them. This is hard to do when going around a curve. At a curve the seamstress must leave the needle in the

fabric, lift the sewing machine foot, turn the project just a little, put the foot back down, and resume zig-zagging. The seamstress must do this several times per curve. This is called pivoting. It keeps the zig-zags close to one another without leaving spaces. Anyway, how this applies to carving is that one day I was fighting with these single line circles. I could not get smoothly in and out of the grain with the inner cut. Suddenly I thought of applique and how I pivoted around the curves. I tried the same technique with carving. It worked!

I let the grain take the knife with it when it wants to, until the knife came to the outer line. Then I went back and picked up the same angle and went on until the grain took my knife with it again. I kept doing this around the parts of the circle that went in and out of the grain. This technique makes carving any curved line easier and smoother. Try this technique. I know it can help.

To execute a curved cut, first make a stop cut on either side of the circle with the grain (Photo 144). Carve the outside curve (or convex side) of the line first (Photo 145). Hold the knife straight up when carving the outward curve. A rule to remember is the tighter the curve, the straighter the knife. I always try to carve the convex side first.

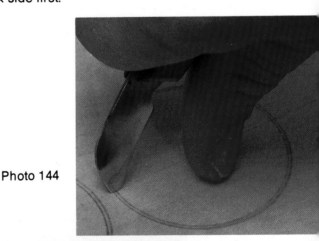

Photo 144

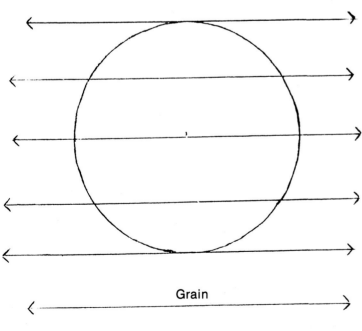

Grain

Drawing 37

Photo 145

Make the second cut on the inside (or concave) side of the line. Lay the knife over a little more to make the second cut. (Photo 146) Think about the point of the knife inside the wood. The two cuts have to meet at the bottom. (Photo 147) If the knife is straight up for the first cut, it lays over just a bit for the second cut, so the two cuts can meet in the wood. (Photo 148)

Two things to remember about carving curved lines; carve the convex side of the line first when possible, and the tighter the curve, the straighter the knife is.

Now, having said that, I have to tell you that there is one instance when you do not want to carve the outer side first. It is when two curved lines meet at a single point, such as this. (Drawing 38) This usually occurs when one carves a picture (not a geometric). This could be the point of a leaf, a beak, a wing tip, etc. Make Cut 1 on the convex side of the top line (Drawing 39). Start at the point and gently insert the knife (Photo 149) and come down the line (Photo 150). Make Cut 2 on the concave side of that line moving toward the point (Photo 151). Straighten the knife at the end of the cut (Photo 152). Execute Cut 3 moving toward the point (Photo 153). Making this cut in this direction first allows the lines to join at the top without risking undercutting the center. It makes a much cleaner, sharper point at the top. Remember to straighten the knife at the point (Photo 154). Start Cut 4 at the top (Photo 155) and move toward your body (Photo 156).

Be patient when practicing this exercise. Once you start getting the technique, it comes quickly. Clean, sharp lines enhance any chip carved design. (Photo 157)

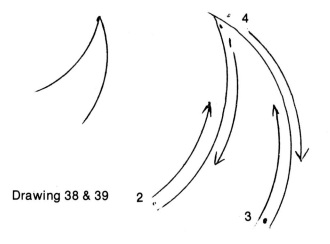

Photo 148: The finished curved line

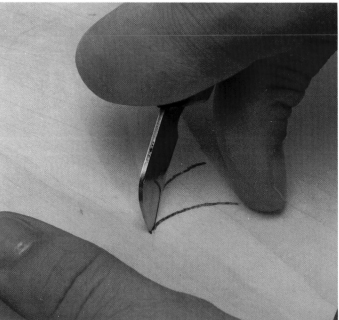

Drawing 38 & 39

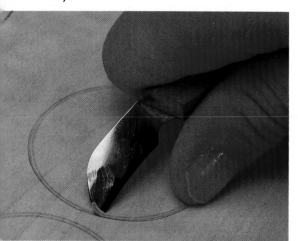

Photo 146

Photo 147

Photo 149

50

Photo 150

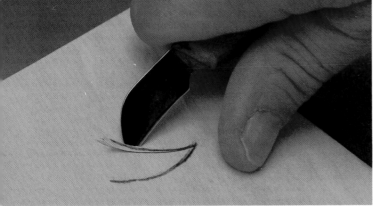

Photo 151

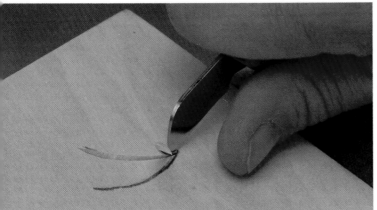

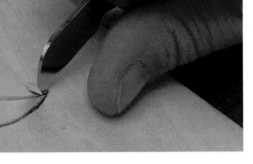

Photo 152

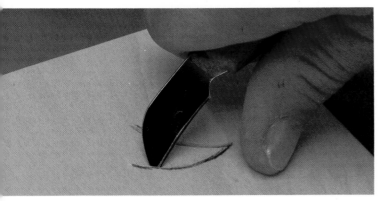

Photo 153

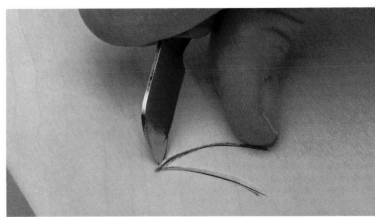

Photo 154

Photo 155

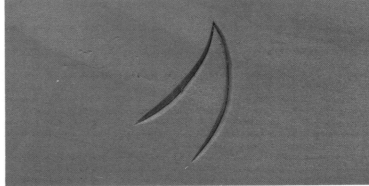

Photo 156

Photo 157

Basic Design Concepts
Finding Center

Rectangles and Squares

Finding center is easy if the piece is in the shape of a rectangle or square. Measure the distance from one side to the other, divide that distance in half. If the piece is out of square, the perpendicular lines derived from this process will not have four right (90 degree) angles. They are not sufficient to draw a rosette. Therefore, draw one center line, either horizontal or vertical, and draw the perpendicular line from the instructions pertaining specifically to that process.

Circles

This is my procedure for finding the center of a circle. I learned it through trial and error. There may be a better way. I know that woodworking catalogs, etc. sell center finders. If you have one—great. If not you might want to follow these instructions. The following seems like a hit and miss method, but I find it works well for me.

Place the grain horizontally in front of you. Find what looks to be center by measuring from edge to edge. (Photo 158) Divide this distance in half and make a small mark. Do the same vertically and make a small mark. Put the point of the compass on the point where they cross. Adjust the compass to some spot on the edge of the circle. Move the pencil end of the compass around the circle to see if it hits all edges. (Photo 159) See which way you need to move the compass point to hit all parts of the edge of the circle. This is an adjustment game here. Moving the point of the compass, and the adjustment, around until you find the center. Mark it with a dot. Many pieces are not true circles. Some plates, for instance, might be just a little shorter one way than the other. Do the best you can and it will look fine when finished.

Now look at the grain. Draw a line parallel with the grain that runs through the center dot you made. (Photo 160) Draw the perpendicular line from the dot on this line. Be sure to make the original line on the same plane as the grain. This will keep the project from looking crooked when finished.

Photo 159

Photo 158

Photo 160

Drawing Perpendicular Lines

To draw a perpendicular line from any given line:

1. Put the point of the compass on the center point. (Drawing 40a)
2. Adjust the compass so it measures approximately ¾ inch out. (Drawing 40b)
3. Strike a small mark on both sides of center. (Photo 161)
4. Lift the point of the compass out, and readjust it to a wider setting.
5. Place the point of the compass on one mark, and draw two arcs. One above the line and one below the line. Do the same from the other mark. (Drawing 40c)(Photo 162)
6. Lay a ruler on the intersections of the two arcs. Draw the line. (Drawing 40d)(Photo 163)
7. Erase the arcs and the small marks on the center line so they do not interfere when you put the design on the board.

Photo 162

1.

Drawing 40a

2&3.

Drawing 40b

6.

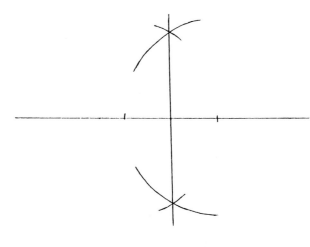

Drawing 40d

Photo 161

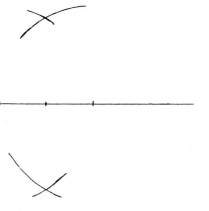

Drawing 40c

Photo 163

Tracing the Designs

To trace a design onto a project you need the following items; parchment paper, erasable tracing paper, tape, and a mechanical pencil. First, lay a piece of parchment paper over the design. Tape the paper to keep it from slipping. Mark the center and crossing lines first so if the paper slips you can easily match it back to the design. Now trace the design onto the parchment paper. Use a ruler to trace any straight lines. A ruler is the only way to keep the lines perfectly straight. A chip carving is only as good as the drawn design.

After you have traced the design onto the parchment paper, remove the paper and place on the board. Match the cross lines. Tape the paper in place on the wood (Photo 164). Next, slide the tracing paper between the parchment paper and the wood. Be sure the marking side of the tracing paper is face down on the wood. Trace the design onto the piece. Use the ruler again to trace the any straight lines (Photo 165). Remove the parchment and tracing paper. Draw any straight lines that need to be drawn at this time. On some patterns I only show marks that indicate the connecting points for straight lines. I do this to keep the precision in the drawing. You are ready to carve a traced design. (Photo 166)

Photo 165: Always trace straight lines with a ruler.

Photo 164

Photo 166

Drawing a Six-Sided Rosette

1. Draw the perpendicular lines. (Drawing 41a)
2. Make a mark 1″ from center on any line.
3. Put the point of the compass in the center and adjust it to the 1″ mark. Draw the circle.
4. Put the point of the compass on point 1. Draw an arc. (Drawing 41b)
5. Where the arc crosses the circle, place the point of your compass and draw another arc. Continue drawing arcs around the circle in this way, until you have created a six-sided rosette. (Drawing 41c)

Six-sided Rosette with Diamonds

5. Draw lines connecting points at ends of ovals. (Drawing 42d)
6. Adjust the compass to the ½″ mark. Strike off the center of the ovals. (Drawing 42e)
7. Mark ⅛″ out from the cross lines in the center of the ovals, for the ends of the diamonds. (Drawing 42f)
8. Mark the diamonds. (Drawing 42g)

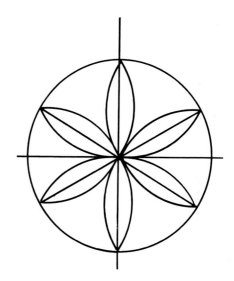

Drawing 42d

Drawing 42e

Drawing 42f

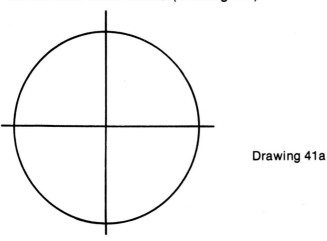

Drawing 41a

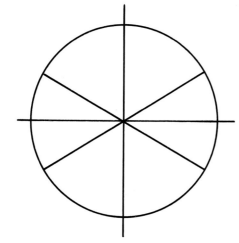

Drawing 41b

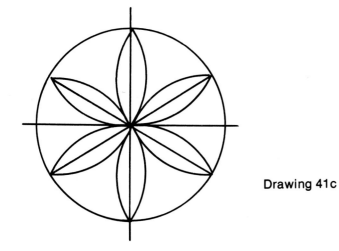

Drawing 41c

Drawing 42g

Drawing Borders

After measuring the board and finding center, one must decide what the ratio of the border and the design will be to the entire piece.

Drawing Metric Borders

The measurements are as follows for those who wish to draw a border in the metric system. I felt this explanation necessary because, being a European art, one usually finds chip carving measured using this system. I wanted to give the reader a frame of reference for this system. Measure the horizontal line spacing in centimeters with spaces of 2, 4, 4, and 2 cm. (Drawing 43) The perpendicular division lines are 4 centimeters apart. (Drawing 44) There is nothing in the decimal system that makes a border quite like this. The closest would be to measure like the one in Drawing 45. When one compares the metric measurements with these, they look about the same. But, when one lays the entire border out this way they seem too close. That is a personal opinion.

I prefer to draw most borders in the metric system. I know I did not teach Exercise One in the metric system, but I felt it too confusing. As I stated there, my concerns were the execution techniques. I did not want the reader/student to quit due to the frustration of too many new ideas at once.

Use whatever system you are comfortable with and like. The only criteria is to divide the borders in equal measurements.

Once the lines are on the board, always draw the borders from the center.

Drawing 43

Drawing 44

Drawing 45

Patterns

I try to develop patterns that appeal to different tastes. Sometimes I carve patterns that to me are "the Americanization of chip carving." By this I mean that the subject of the pattern in strictly American, but the manner of execution finds its roots in the European style. These incised patterns, such as sailboats, dogwood blossoms, detailed animals, and Southwestern designs reflect an American taste. I call them incised carvings, rather than chip carvings. The pattern, not created by removing a regular, precise series of chips, does not fit the definition of chip carving. They use the same techniques though.

The most attractive and curious aspect to me is the absence of limitation of design. The chip carver that learns and practices the proper technique, can carve almost any design that ones' mind can imagine. The more I carve, and understand how to use the knife, the faster new and better designs come to me. I still like to use many traditional designs. When I see a design in many American books, books from foreign countries, and on older pieces such as butter molds, boxes, and furniture, I consider it to be traditional. I enjoy carving them because of their tradition. I like carving as I know people have for centuries before me.

I also enjoy combining the old with the new. I love to design new patterns as much as I love to carve. New ideas and designs keep the excitement in chip carving. I have literally carved thousands of pieces, and I have not tired of chip carving yet. I find it more challenging as time goes on. I am always striving to become more innovative and faster, and to improve my technique. Chip carving gives me a great sense of accomplishment. I hope it does the same for you.

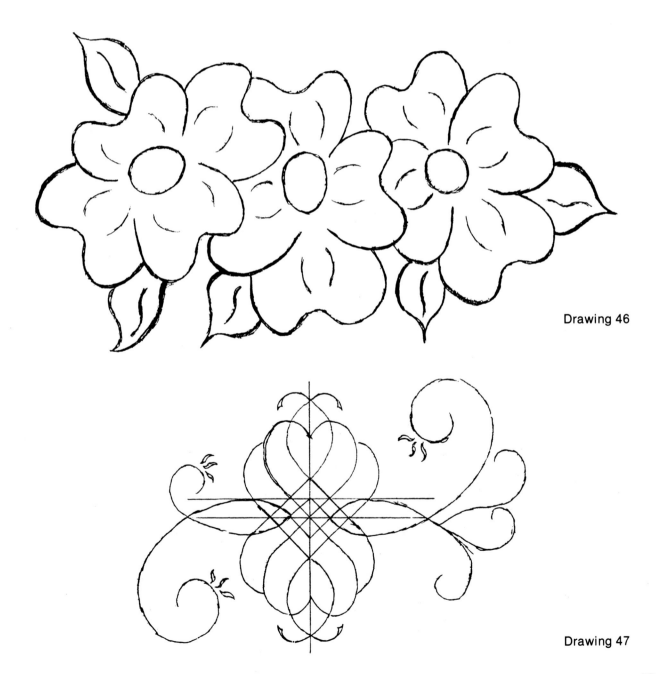

Drawing 46

Drawing 47

Normally I would draw the border before drawing the center, but in this project the border was an afterthought added at the end. I would strongly recommend drawing the border before carving the center.

Drawing 48: Find the center of the plate and draw or copy a pattern on it. Be sure that you are centered and that one of the main lines of the pattern goes with the grain.

Carving a Platter

Start at the center of the pattern and carve the triangles.

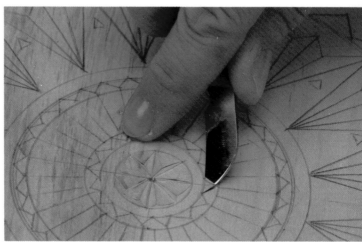

knife position 2 for the second...

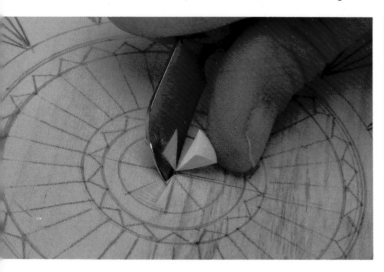

With three cuts each triangle should pop right out.

Move to the next ring of triangles and carve the ones pointing out. Use knife position 1 for the first cut...

and knife position 1 for the final cut. Continue around the pattern.

The first two areas carved.

Cut stops at the ends of the radiating lines, first on the inside...

Turn the piece and go the other way. Continue around the pattern.

Then on the outer end.

Now go back and carve the circle at the base of those lines. Start with the outside cut.

Carve the straight lines using knife position one in each direction.

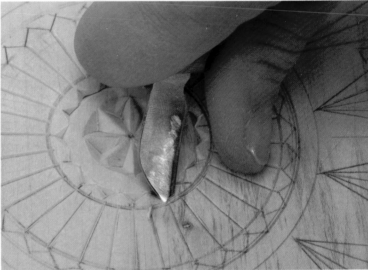

Go back and do the inside.

Cut the triangles at the outside. Cut 1 in knife position 1.

With the knife in position 1 begin to carve the adjacent triangles. Start at the point with your knife just slightly into the wood.

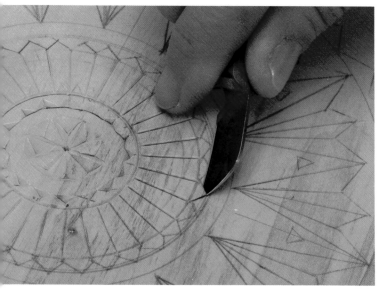

Knife position 2 for cut 2.

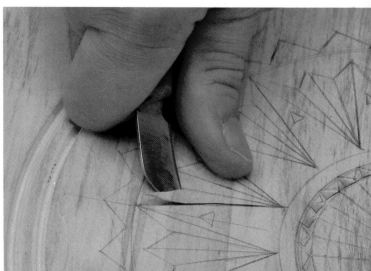

Carve the back at the short end of the triangle, also using knife position 1.

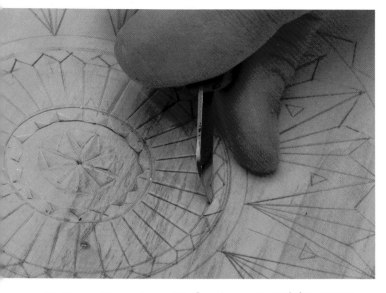

Knife position 1 for cut 3. Continue around the pattern.

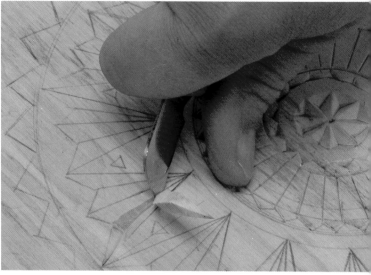

Carve back to the point. The triangle should pop out.

Repeat the process with the adjacent triangle, starting at the point...

Its getting a little crowded at the point, so don't go right into it with the next cut. Start a little bit out and carve lightly at the beginning of the cut.

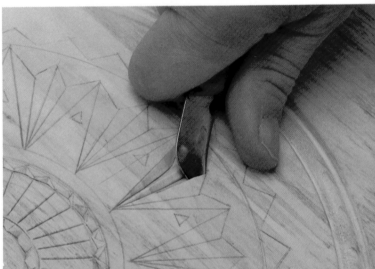

Carving the end...

Move deeper toward the end.

Carving back to the point.

Continue with the end cut...

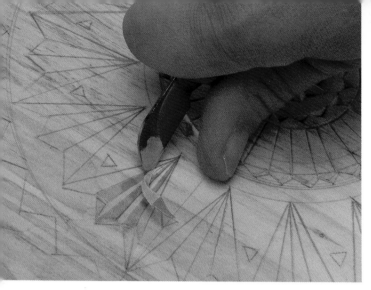

And back to the point.

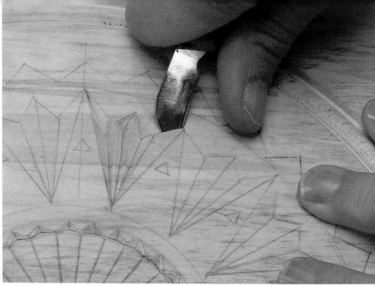

Cut across the end...

The final triangle begins again at the point,

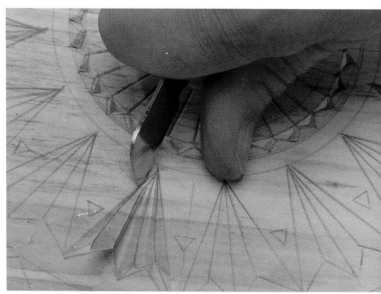

and back to the point. This completes the first set of adjacent triangles.

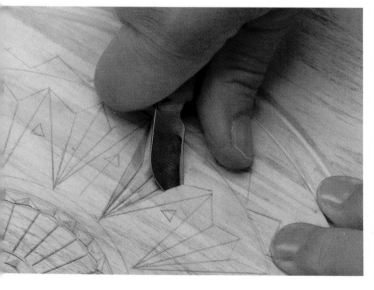

and gets deeper toward the end.

Continue around the pattern until you get to this point.

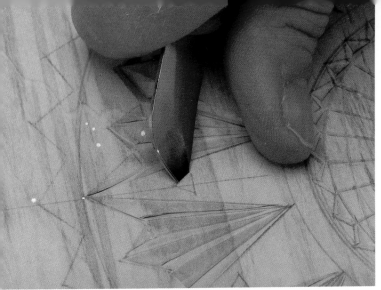

The triangles between the adjacent triangles are formed with three simple cuts. One...

This takes you to this stage.

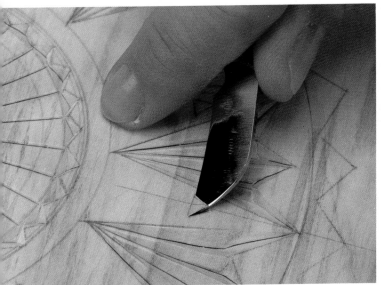

Two...

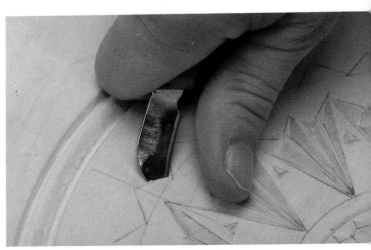

Move to the next ring of triangles. Cut 1 is in knife position 1.

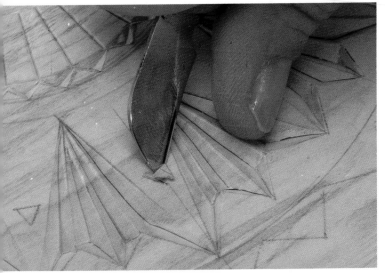

Three

Cut 2, knife position 2.

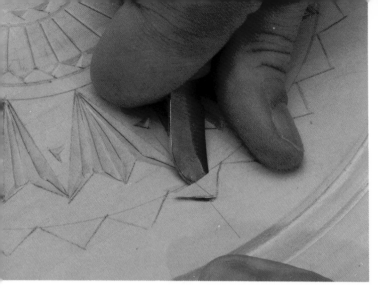

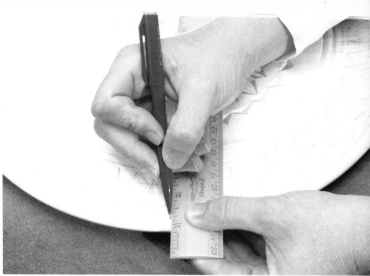

Cut 3, knife position 1.

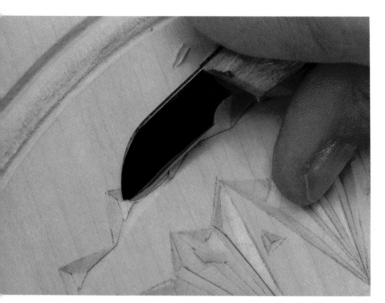

If you find a little bit left at the bottom of the triangle follow the same angles and clean it out.

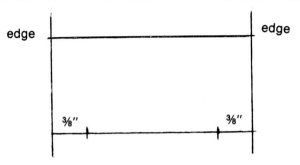

Let me take you through the process step by step. The border pattern we will use combines two patterns we have practiced earlier. Begin by laying your ruler through the center and measuring ⅜″ in from the edge of the platter and marking it. (Drawing 49)

You can see how the pattern is developing. This is the end of the transferred pattern.

The inside line depends on the plate you have. When my plates are made a beaded circle is made on the lathe to separate the rim from the center. From there I measure ⅜″ toward the outside and mark again. If you don't have a bead like that you can measure from the center or do all your measuring from the outside edge.

65

and finally the middle circle.

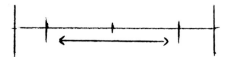

Find the point half way between these two points with your compass and mark it. (Drawing 50)

Measure in ⅛″ in from the outside circle...

Use the compass to mark the circles around the plate, first the outside circle...

then the inside circle...

and ⅛″ out from the inside circle and mark each point (Drawing 51). Now mark the point that is halfway between these ⅛″ marks and the middle circle (Drawing 52).

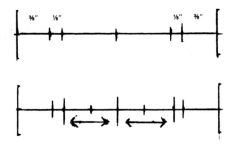

Return to the compass and draw circles through these points.

and through inward point.

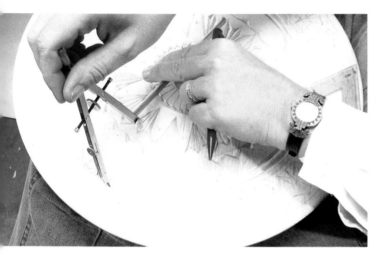

Your plate border probably will not measure the same as this one. Using the measuring technique described, it is not necessary that they be the same. You can measure in from each edge any distance you want. Once you have the two outside lines on one edge (one for the outside single line and one for the actual carved border edge) the distance between the inner lines is just divided into equal amounts, i.e. halved, then quartered. Use a compass to draw the circles.

Laying your ruler through the center of the plate and the points of the ring of triangles that is the outside ring of the middle of the plate. Draw a line across the rim on a radius that goes each outward point in the triangle circle...

With the protractor draw an arc from where one line intersects the sixth circle to where the next line intersects the third circle. Do the same thing in each direction, working your way around the rim. Skipping every other line you end up with a nice pattern of rounded triangle.

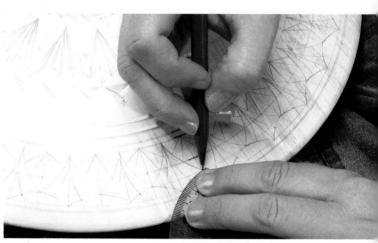

From the point of the rounded triangle, use your protractor again to draw another arc to the intersection of the radius line and the second circle. This creates a ring of fans between the rounded triangles.

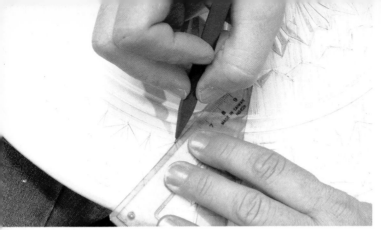

From the center of the base of the triangles, draw straight lines to where the circles meet their sides.

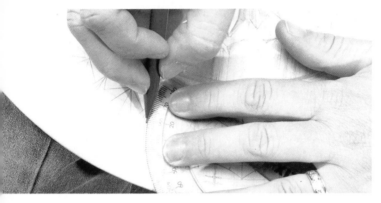

Use the protractor to divide the fans into four curved segments. The pattern you end up with should look something like Drawing 52, though the dimensions may differ

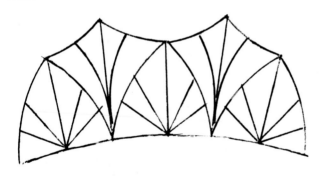

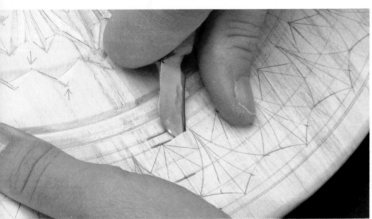

Finally you get to cut. Begin at the center of the triangle base and cut out toward the edge.

Cut 2

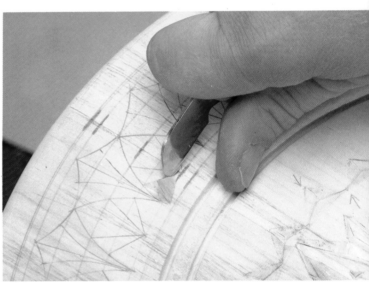

Cut 3

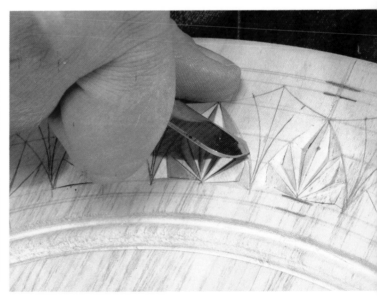

Work your way around each rounded triangle.

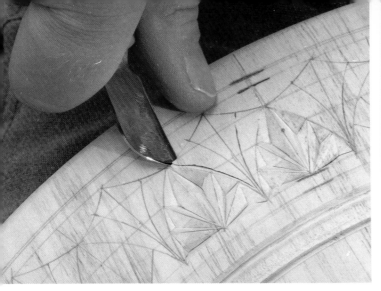

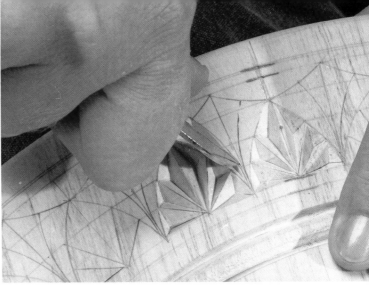

Begin carving the fan with cut 1 along the outside edge and cut 2 across the short side.

Continue with the next segment of the fan. This is the start of cut 1, with the blade lightly inserted.

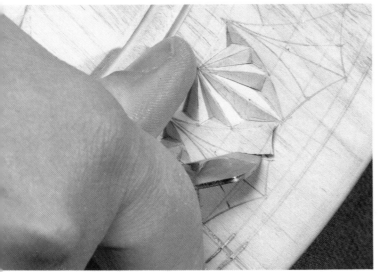

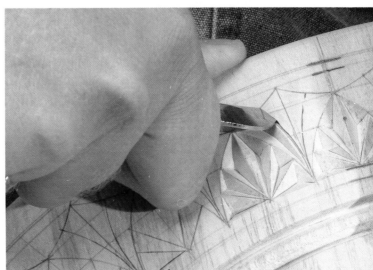

Complete the line of the triangle cutting toward the point.

At the end of cut 1 the knife is deeper.

The piece should pop out.

Cut 2.

Cut 3.

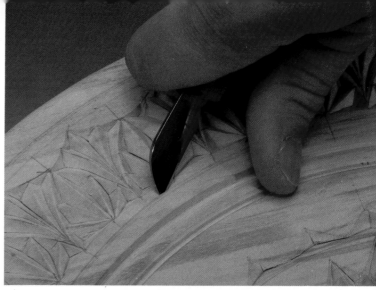

First carve one way in knife position 1.

The rim pattern completed.

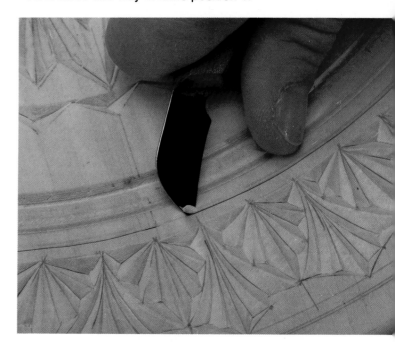

Then turn the plate and carve in the other direction, still using knife position 1.

Two curved lines will finish the plate. Start with a stop cut.

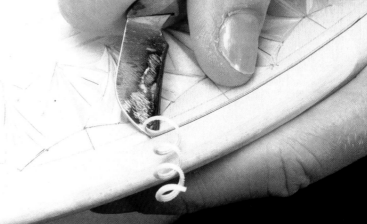

If you're lucky you'll get a nice curly strip of waste wood as you carve.

The finished plate.

Gallery of Designs

73

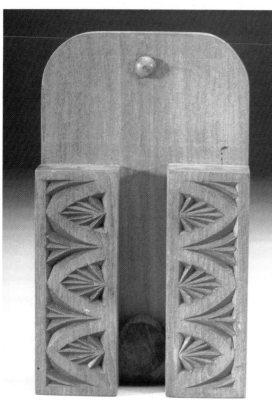

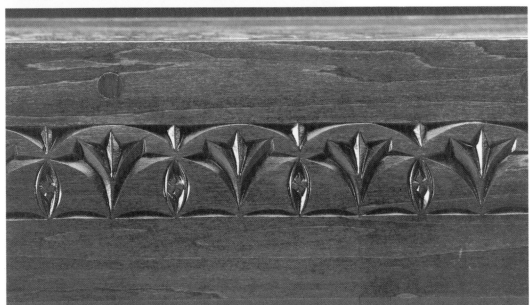